THE COMPLETE BOOK
OF CHILD CUSTODY

Also by the author

TEACHING YOUR CHILD TO COPE WITH CRISIS

THE
COMPLETE BOOK
OF
CHILD CUSTODY

SUZANNE RAMOS

G. P. PUTNAM'S SONS
New York

LIBRARY OF CONGRESS CATALOGING IN PUBLICATION DATA

Ramos, Suzanne.
  The Complete Book of Child Custody.
    Bibliography: p.
    1. Children of Divorced Parents—United States.
    2. Custody of Children—United States.
      I. Title.
    HQ777.5.R35   1979   301.42'8   78-26061

ISBN 0-399-12204-4

Printed in the United States of America

ACKNOWLEDGMENTS

I would like to express my deep thanks to the authorities whom I interviewed at length. They contributed thoughtfully and generously. My thanks, too, to those whose research I studied. Because I generally did not include their credentials in the text of the book, I list them here:

Barry N. Berger; Attorney; New York City

Katherine Cobb, Ph.D.; Clinical psychologist and child therapist; New York City

Stanley Cohen, Ph.D.; Sociologist; Faculty, University of Oregon Medical Center

Frank Curran, M.D.; Consulting psychiatrist, St. Luke's Hospital, New York City; Retired Professor of Psychiatry and Neurology, University of Virginia Medical Center

André Derdeyn, M.D.; Faculty, Department of Psychiatry, University of Virginia Medical Center

David Fanshel, Ph.D.; Professor, Columbia University School of Social Work

5

Acknowledgments

Marie Friedman, M.D.; Director of Inpatient Adolescent Services at Long Island Jewish Hillside Medical Center

Richard A. Gardner, M.D.; Assistant Clinical Professor of Psychiatry, College of Physicians and Surgeons, Columbia University; Faculty, William A. White Psychoanalytic Institute; Author, *The Boys and Girls Book About Divorce* and other books, and most recently, *The Boys and Girls Book About One-Parent Families*

Hon. Justice Bentley Kassal; Member of the Supreme Court, New York County

Joan B. Kelly, Ph.D.; Marin County Mental Health Center, San Rafael, California; Co-principal investigator, Children of Divorce Project

Clarice J. Kestenbaum, M.D.; Director of Child and Adolescent Psychiatry, St. Luke's Hospital Center, New York City; Associate Clinical Professor of Psychiatry, College of Physicians and Surgeons, Columbia University

Alan Levy, M.D.; Chief of Child and Adolescent Psychiatric Services, Beth Israel Medical Center, New York City; Associate Clinical Professor of Psychiatry, Mt. Sinai School of Medicine, New York City

Brinkley Long, M.A.; Director, Family Court Services, Sacramento County, Sacramento, California

Marcia Lowry; Attorney; Director, Children's Rights Project, New York Civil Liberties Union

John Money, Ph.D.; Professor of Medical Psychology, Professor of Psychiatry, Professor of Pediatrics; The Johns Hopkins School of Medicine

Ann Parks; Parents Without Partners, Inc., Bethesda, Maryland

Richard B. Pesikoff, M.D.; Assistant Professor of Psychiatry, Division of Child Psychiatry, Baylor College of Medicine, Houston, Texas

Acknowledgments

Hon. Judge Justine Wise Polier; Retired Member of the Family Court, New York County

Sally Provence, M.D.; Professor of Pediatrics, Yale University Child Study Center

Hon. Judge Cesar Quinones; Member of the Family Court, New York County

Robert Ravich, M.D.; Clinical Associate Professor of Psychiatry, Cornell University Medical School

Hon. Judge Guy G. Ribaudo; Member of the Civil Court, New York County

Edward R. Ritvo, M.D.; Professor, Division of Mental Retardation and Child Psychiatry, UCLA Medical School

Miriam Robinson, Attorney; New York City; Vice-President, American Academy of Matrimonial Lawyers

Sirgay Sanger, M.D.; Director, Parent-Child Program, St. Luke's Hospital, New York City; Instructor of Psychiatry, College of Physicians and Surgeons, Columbia University; Author, *Emotional Care of Hospitalized Children*

Albert Solnit, M.D.; Sterling Professor of Pediatrics and Psychiatry, and Director, Yale University Child Study Center; Co-author, *Beyond the Best Interests of the Child*

Philip F. Solomon, Attorney; New York City; Past President, American Academy of Matrimonial Lawyers

Judith S. Wallerstein, M.S.W.; School of Social Welfare, University of California, Berkeley, California; Co-principal Investigator, Children of Divorce Project

Andrew S. Watson, M.D.; Professor of Law and Psychiatry, University of Michigan

I also spoke with mothers, fathers and children (some of whom are adults, some adolescents, some still young children) who have had years of personal experience with custody. They offered me numerous key insights, without which I could not have written this book, and I

7

Acknowledgments

sincerely thank them all for going into an intimate subject and enriching the book with real life.

For repeated interviews, for reading parts of my manuscript, or for otherwise being exceptionally helpful in its completion, my gratitude goes again to Dr. Gardner and attorney Berger, to Laurie Tag at G. P. Putnam's, and to my husband, Joseph Ramos.

Special thanks for her valuable editorial contributions to Barbara Wyden, my editor.

S.R.
October, 1978

To John and Julie

CONTENTS

11

Contents

12

Contents

13

Contents

14

Contents

Contents

16

Contents

17

Contents

18

THE COMPLETE BOOK
OF CHILD CUSTODY

IN THEIR OWN BEST INTERESTS
A Fable for Parents

On April 21, 1978, Steven Jones filed a custody suit in New York County Supreme Court. In his petition, Mr. Jones asked for custody of his two parents, Martin, forty, and Gail, thirty-five. He stated that he wished them to reside with him and his younger sister, Eileen, on a full-time basis at 680 East 51 Street in New York City. The basis of his suit, Jones explained, is that the emotional climate created by "split" parents is an unhealthy one for children. As evidence, he cited his own and his sister's unhappiness, his failing grades in mathematics and French, his sister's temper tantrums, "which she has at least twice a day," and the fact that he bites his finger-nails.

Jones, who is ten years old, is being represented by Marcia Barrett, a well-known attorney in the field of children's rights. "Where did you get the money to retain

Ms. Barrett?" Jones was asked by one of the group of reporters who had gathered around him and his lawyer outside the courthouse.

"Fortunately, I've saved all my birthday, Christmas, Easter and Valentine's gifts from my grandparents," he replied. "Children should always have some money of their own for a legal retainer because lawyers don't like to take on a case and wait to see if the judge will make the parents pay the bill. We, as children, have to become more aware of how we can protect our interests."

"You have your own attorney. Do you favor your parents having their own legal counsel?" asked a journalist from the *Times*.

"I don't think that will be necessary," he answered. "We have their best interests at heart."

"If you do win this case, Mr. Jones," another reporter asked, "will you permit visiting privileges for your mother's boyfriend and your father's second wife?"

"I'll give that careful thought," he said, "but, according to the psychiatric consultation I had, that would be giving them a double message and would probably be very confusing to them."

"Have you consulted your parents as to their wishes on this?" he was asked.

"My sister and I have talked to them, but we feel we can't put too much stock in any living arrangement they request. Last year they wanted to live together. Then they wanted to live by themselves. Now they want to live with other people. Who knows what they'll want next year? In this case, we'll have to decide what's best for them."

"Suppose your parents aren't happy together? Suppose they have problems adjusting?"

"We'll get professional help. Eileen and I feel that it's important for them to work through their feelings and to talk about any anger they are experiencing. And we'll give them a lot of love. After that," Jones continued, "I feel that if my sister and I set clear limits from the start, they will learn to cope with each other.

"After all," he went on, "we feel that's part of being a parent."

PART ONE

CUSTODY TO THE PRESENT DAY

Chapter One

UNLESS AND UNTIL . . .

The average child takes his life and custody very much for granted. He will be loved, cared for, protected, and prepared for life by two devoted parents from his birth to his maturity. Why two parents? In the words of one social historian, "The two-parent nuclear family is ideally suited for raising children." Or, as a seven-year-old boy said, "Two parents are better than one."

Unless . . . they fight, threaten, lie, stay out nights, drink too much, and otherwise make themselves and each other consistently unhappy and cause their children to be nervous, withdrawn, angry, or unable to function. Then, one parent may be better than two. Living with one parent in a stable home falls somewhere in the middle between the ideal of having two parents who love each other and their children and the tragic situation of living with two parents who are at war with one another.

Close to one in five American children live in one-parent families today. It is very possible for these families to be happy and self-sufficient—the children well-adjusted and contented to live with that parent. But there are emotional traps that often preclude children's healthy adjustment. For the child of divorce, a bitter court battle, intense loyalty conflicts, a parent too depressed or distracted to provide the necessary emotional support, or a home atmosphere tense with anger left over from the marriage, can stand in the way of his normal development. These situations arise where parents continue to argue long after the separation, use a child to spy on his other parent, or try to turn a child against his other parent.

With the high number of marriages breaking up over the past decade, divorce has recently been called "the greatest social dislocation of our time." Because divorce represents a revolution in the way an enormous number of parents and their children are living, child custody has become an issue of staggering magnitude. There are well over one million divorces a year in the United States, more than double the rate of ten years ago and 700 percent above the rate at the turn of the century. In trend-setting Los Angeles, there are more than 1,000 divorces a week. Half of them involve children under the age of fourteen. Add to this the fact that in any given year the number of marital separations roughly *equals* the number of divorces, and we begin to appreciate the millions of children in each year who are joining the ranks of a new class—those growing up in single-parent homes—those who must deal with the feelings of loss, grief, and confusion that come with separation and divorce. Quite naturally, the parents of these children worry about how they can best handle their youngsters throughout this difficult time.

Unless and Until. . .

During a separation, a parent's most urgent wishes concerning her or his children are: to demonstrate that, in spite of everything, he or she still loves them; to relieve some of the intense guilt the parent feels about the family breaking up; to do what is right for the children; and, above all, to retain their love.

Most parents think no more about custody than their children do. They take it for granted that they will manage jointly the physical, emotional and intellectual responsibilities that come with raising children. But when a marriage goes bad, suddenly custody looms as an ominous burden. Each parent must face having it alone, not having it at all, or working out a cooperative, sharing arrangement which will not upset their child or children further—a difficult task for people whose emotions may be so raw that they are unable to communicate with one another rationally. "Nothing is more acutely sensitive," comments one lawyer, "than the relationship between two people who no longer want to share each other's lives."

This is the time when parents themselves are most vulnerable and it is most difficult for them to act or even think logically and rationally. In the midst of their own distress, they must prepare for their child's troubled feelings about the separation. Emotionally unsteady, parents must make definite plans for the child's welfare. The custody arrangements have to be worked out and carefully explained to the child. As much order or routine as possible must be kept in the disrupted household, an unpredictable spouse must be kept at bay, and preparations for a new life for everyone must be begun.

Parents would be better able to ease the emotional strain of separation and divorce on children if they knew more about the psychological impact on children of

29

parental separation; if they understood just what the emotional and mental effects of legal hassling over custody and visitation were; if they were more sensitive to the long- and short-term effects on children of the separation of a child from his parent, prolonged parental conflict, parents' moods, and other signs of stress.

This book discusses custody and its ramifications for children. It is written especially for parents and for those professionals who might find it useful in their work with parents and children. Many parents who have lived through the dramatic ups and downs as well as the daily pressures of separation and divorce as they relate to the custody of children have shared their experiences, their feelings and their thoughts for this book. Leading child psychiatrists and psychologists have detailed their work with children of divorce and their research on the effects of divorce and custody. And judges and attorneys have discussed custody laws as well as how the courts and the legal process can affect the children and adults who must deal with custody.

There is no perfect custody arrangement and there are no easy solutions for raising children of divorce. Yet there are general patterns that have emerged and constructive approaches that can help parents handle this difficult problem, so far-reaching in its consequences for their children's future well-being.

I hope this unbiased account of the personal experiences of many families as well as the latest research findings on the subject will make divorce and custody easier on children and parents.

Chapter Two

CUSTODY, A LOOK BACK

To better understand the opinions on custody held by leading judges, psychiatrists, and lawyers today, it might be helpful to look back at how our thinking has evolved concerning families, divorce, and custody.

In the last hundred years, children, who had been considered in the eyes of the law nothing more than property like cows and cars, have become individuals with rights and needs understood and protected by law.

Custody in the Nineteenth Century

Until well into the nineteenth century most children were treated much the same as servants. Often young children worked on their fathers' farms from dawn until dusk. Before child labor laws began to appear in the mid-1800s, many children as young as five or six worked in factories for long days and low wages, sometimes supporting their entire families if their fathers were unemployed.

In the 4 to 5 percent of American marriages which ended in divorce at that time, custody generally went to fathers because in an agricultural society where men owned the property and lived by farming the land, children were valuable economic resources. Mothers were not permitted to take children away from their fathers, nor did they have the financial means to oppose the existing system.

The courts consistently and often in the face of compelling evidence to the contrary, upheld the paramount right of fathers to custody of their children. In 1857, Mrs. Humphries went to court in New York State seeking a separation from her husband and custody of their child. The judge in the case acknowledged that the evidence showed that Mr. Humphries was "unkind and disrespectful to his wife and had often used vulgar language to her and to others about her." Nevertheless the judge stated that the husband "had been guilty of no such misconduct as would justify the wife in a separation." The judge ruled that the father's right to custody would stand and that Mrs. Humphries had no option but to stay with her husband or to leave without her child. "The only difficulty arises from the child being of tender age and deriving its sustenance in part from the breasts of the mother," the judge said, "but I think these circumstances form no obstacle to the father's right."[1]

In later nineteenth-century America there were a few instances of mothers obtaining custody of their children, especially where the woman was able to convince a conservative-minded judge that her husband held atheistic or other "immoral" beliefs. But at that time there was no such thing as child support. In the rare case where a mother did win custody, the courts generally ruled that since a father's support for his child was given in exchange for the child's labor, "a father is no longer liable for the support of his minor child after the custody of his minor child has been given to the mother."[2]

The Beginnings of Change for Women

During the late nineteenth and early twentieth centuries the country was undergoing major shifts. The rural society was becoming predominantly industrial. Many men left the farms for jobs in the cities. Women's roles were changing too. Significant numbers of women began to work for pay, some owned property, and in 1919, fifty years after the Fourteenth Amendment guaranteed men the right to vote, the Susan B. Anthony Federal Suffrage Amendment—the Nineteenth Amendment—was passed, giving the vote to women.

With less need for hands to work the fields and a premium on space in the cities where the jobs were, parents had fewer children and paid more attention to each child's needs.

Society did more for children as well. Public education improved, child labor became more stringent. At about the time that greater numbers of men and women were *competing* for the same jobs in factories rather than *cooperating* in a joint effort as they had on the farms, men as well as society in general embraced the idea that the mother-child relationship is a key to a child's healthy emotional development and that mothers should be at home with, and in the event of divorce, have custody of, their young children. Psychological principles concerning the importance of a loving, consistent mother figure in the development of children's basic trust became the rationale for what was to be called the "tender-years doctrine."

The tender-years doctrine began as a belief that a very young child needed his mother's regular care. It was first used only to justify a temporary interruption to the father's right to custody as in the case of a thirteen-year-old Virginia girl who stayed with her mother following her parents' separation until, at the age of four, it was ruled by a judge to be best that she go to live permanently with her father because "the tender nursing period has passed by and the time for moral training and impressions has arrived."[3]

However, as fewer fathers were operating farms for which they needed their children's labor, as mothers' rights gained strength, and as psychological principles were more widely accepted, the tender-years theory became the basis for permanent custody being given to mothers in an increasing number of cases. In some states, laws were officially passed favoring custody awards of all children under twelve to mothers.

New court rulings and laws appeared around the turn of the century which required fathers, *for the first time,* to provide financial support for their children even if the children were not in their fathers' custody. This child-support provision represented a turning point in women's ability to assume custody.

Some judges became emotional about the importance of a mother's care. "There is but a twilight zone between a

34

mother's love and the atmosphere of heaven. All other things being equal no child should be deprived of that maternal influence,"[4] wrote one.

The Best Interests of the Child

Soon after the tender-years doctrine became widely accepted, a new standard, labeled the "best interests of the child" theory, appeared in custody decisions written by two forward looking judges. The best-interests standard was a turning point for children's rights in custody matters because for the first time, the *welfare of the child* came before the rights of either the mother or the father.

Judge Benjamin Cardozo, who was said to have converted the United States Supreme Court from a court of law to a court of justice, set many legal precedents. As a New York Court of Appeals judge in 1925, ruling on a child custody case, he wrote a landmark decision stating that in custody cases the judge is not there to decide whether father or mother has a cause for action against the other but rather, the judge "acts as *parens patriae* to do what is best for the interests of the child. He is to put himself in the position of a wise, affectionate, and careful parent and make provisions for the child accordingly,"[5] even where this means superseding a parent's natural right to custody.

The best-interests concept, though vague, suggested for the first time that a child has rights and needs independent of those of his parents and that it is not only in children's interests but in society's long-range interests to raise healthy citizens and, therefore, to make custody decisions based on children's needs.

35

Although more enlightened than the tender-years doctrine, in practice the "best interests of the child" principle did not have an immediate impact. Long-standing tradition and the bias of most judges saw custody decisions continue to favor mothers for many years in all but the most extreme cases. Unless a father could prove that his child had an unfit mother, meaning a woman who was seriously negligent, sexually promiscuous or dependent on drugs or alcohol, he would have had little chance at custody.

With the growing demand for individual rights and the current sensitivity to discrimination on the basis of sex, the tender-years doctrine has been stricken from the law books of many states on the grounds that it discriminates against men and does not provide them with equal protection of the law.

Leading judges and psychiatrists have also emphasized that with its bias towards mothers it can stand in the way of the only proper criterion for custody, the best interests of the child.

Human prejudice still gives mothers some advantage today but the courts diligently search for a child's best interests in the form of what some experts call his "psychological parent," meaning the adult to whom a child has the closest emotional bond, and, most recently, for what has been labeled "the least detrimental" custody alternative.

The Michigan Criteria for Custody

Possibly the greatest recent advance in custody legislation has been the State of Michigan's Progressive Child

Custody Act of 1970, which spells out ten specific criteria for determining just what a child's best interests are. For the first time judges have specific standards instead of a vague, well-intentioned theory to guide their decisions. These Michigan criteria, which have influenced laws as well as judicial decisions in many other states, are:

1. The love, affection and other emotional ties existing between competing parties and the child.
2. The capacity and disposition of competing parties to give the child love, affection and guidance and continuation of the educating and raising of the child in its religion or creed, if any.
3. The capacity and disposition of competing parties to provide the child with food, clothing, medical care or other remedial care recognized and permitted under the laws of this state in lieu of medical care and other material needs.
4. The length of time the child has lived in a stable, satisfactory environment and the desirability of maintaining continuity.
5. The permanence of the family unit in the existing or proposed custodial home.
6. The moral fitness of the competing parties.
7. The mental and physical health of the competing parties.
8. The home, school and community record of the child.
9. The reasonable preference of the child if the court deems the child to be of sufficient age to express preference.
10. Any other factor considered by the court to be relevant to a particular child's custody dispute."

Although a law such as Michigan's makes decisions easier to reach by going a long way to define best interests, precise definitions still elude us. What is "moral fitness"? Does moral fitness disqualify a woman who has been living with a man for a year, or a man who has lived with three women in twelve months? The caliber of final custody decisions still depends to a great degree on the widely varying skill, training, and open-mindedness of judges and the psychiatrists, psychologists and social workers whom they consult.

While in recent years there have been a great many changes in our thinking regarding custody, in roughly 90 percent of all cases, mothers still get custody of their children, usually as part of an arrangement which both parents agreed to as the best and most practical for all concerned. This still leaves close to a million American children under the age of eighteen who now live with their fathers, 50,000 of these children being of preschool age. Yet, it still remains difficult for fathers to obtain custody.

While mothers still obtain custody of their children in the majority of cases, child-custody decisions, nevertheless, show greater flexibility today than ever before. Deciding on the basis of children's best interests, judges in recent years have made custody awards to fathers over mothers, to stepmothers over natural fathers, grandparents over parents, and to foster and adoptive parents over natural parents.

In a 1977 Supreme Court case in New York County, Judge Bentley Kassal determined that custody of two boys ages fifteen and sixteen should go to their stepmother rather than to their natural father.[7]

Important in Judge Kassal's decision was his finding that "the psychological parent-child relationship in this case is extremely strong," and that in their direct testimony the boys expressed love and gratitude towards their stepmother. "Both consider her to be their mom."

In contrast, he said, the boys "feel abandoned and neglected by their father . . . he left them eight years ago when they were quite young in the custody of their biological mother (now deceased) in California who had a drinking problem and neglected them. He made no serious effort to maintain contact with them during a period of time when they lived with her and he lived in New York . . . they feel doubly abandoned since their father again moved out of their life a year and a half ago without a struggle," when he left them with their stepmother.

Judge Kassal explained that in the preceding year and a half, the father, who is a well-paid executive, had provided no financial support for the boys and had virtually not communicated with them. The boys' resentment towards their father was so strong that they claimed they would have nothing further to do with him regardless of how the court ruled.

The impartial court-appointed psychiatrist who had examined all members of the family stated as part of her recommendation:

The stepmother "has been the nurturing figure in (the boys') otherwise deprived lives and is unquestionably their psychological parent as they are her psychological children. To break this family bond could only have disastrous effects on all three."

Parents Who Don't Want Custody

A recent phenomenon which seems to have contributed to the divorce rate and complicated custody dilemmas is that more and more middle-class women as well as men seem to aspire to financial success and individual fulfillment. The trend among some parents to "do their own thing" is most tragically felt in those families where, following separation, neither parent wants custody of the children.

During the past two decades, increasing numbers of women have become involved in outside careers or other interests and have been reluctant to accept or have refused custody. In some cases, women whose income would make them ineligible for any alimony or child support but would not allow them to support their children comfortably have opted not to take custody. While it is true that men are showing more interest in having custody, this is not occurring in large enough numbers to offset the number of less interested mothers. In fact, while fathers now obtain custody in approximately 10 percent of all family breakups with the rate rising every year, most men still do not seek custody or seem to want it.

A recent sampling by a father of his divorced male acquaintances turned up these reactions to his own decision to take custody of his young teen-age son. One asked, "Do you know what you're letting yourself in for?" Another inquired, "What's wrong with the kid, his mother not able to keep him in line?" And there were several who felt "Children need their mothers" and "Women have a special feeling for children."[x]

Professionals are concerned about the declining interest among some parents in taking on custody and in the tendency for separated and divorced parents to be working or away from home a great deal of the time. "If neither mothers or fathers give the family top priority what will happen to the children?" asks one psychiatrist. He feels that if parents don't live up to their responsibilities to provide the time and love necessary to children's emotional security, "Everyone will pay a price in the end—the children are likely to have emotional difficulties later on and parents will feel remorseful over what they might have done differently."

"Some parents seem to believe that anyone can raise their children," says Dr. Sally Provence of the Yale University Child Study Center. While theoretically it is not harmful to children for both parents to work, even when parents are separated, this assumes that the parents realize that children need a good baby-sitter and that even a good caretaker is not a parent and does not meet certain important emotional needs which only a parent-figure can fulfill. What many parents may not understand is that a key difference between parents and most substitutes is a parent's partiality—one might call it love—for his or her child. Without enough of that crucial partiality, children lose out, especially children of separation and divorce who are already at a disadvantage because they don't see one of their parents as much as they had before the marriage ended.

Some parents who refuse custody entirely or those who accept it in name only and, in fact, turn their children over to a third party, often don't realize how their children feel.

Caroline's parents separated when she was six years old. After two years had passed and they were divorced, they believed that she was adjusting well in spite of the fact that both parents worked full-time in demanding jobs, went out frequently, and took regular business and pleasure trips without the child. While Caroline lived in her mother's home, she spent almost all of her waking time with a competent, but emotionally distant, house-keeper and rarely saw her mother more than one evening a week. Her father usually spent about three hours on Sunday afternoons with her.

One day Caroline brought home a class magazine which her second grade had written. In a section headed "Dear David," the children had "written in" for advice about their personal problems. While most letters sounded something like, "My brother teases me too much. How can I get him to stop bugging me?" or, "I hate homework. It cuts into my baseball time. What should I do?", Caroline's letter read, "Dear David, I hardly ever get to see my mother and father. They are divorced and I know they both are very busy. But I think they could spend a little more time with me. Sometimes I think they don't love me. How can I get to see them more?"

Eight-year-old David's advice was, "Dear Caroline, Tell your mother and father that you are important too and that you like to be with them. Ask them to try harder."

When Caroline's mother showed the magazine to a friend, she told her friend how furious she was at the teacher for having printed the letter and then explained that Caroline was just a little upset because her former nurse had left and "she's not used to this one yet. She'll get over it," her mother explained.

The fact is, fortunately, that the majority of parents who work are very concerned and would like to know more about what effects their working has on their children. This is true particularly of separated and divorced parents, who often are quickest to blame themselves for any problem their children have.

Parental guilt has become common in our culture. With our increased awareness of the effects of the parent-child relationship on children's development, it has become common for any child's problem to be linked to something "in the home." When that home is "broken," it becomes an even easier explanation for a child's aggressiveness, moodiness, poor school work, lack of friends, or other difficulty.

Certainly all problems which children have are not related to parental separation. Some are normal hurdles of growing up and would have occurred regardless of the break. Yet, the "broken home" theory is not groundless. Numerous research studies along with testimony from psychiatrists and educators show children of divorce to be almost twice as likely to develop emotional, academic, and social problems as their counterparts in intact families. Parents today are more likely than those of former years to realize that separation and divorce represent a threat to a child's sense of security, his self-esteem, his ability to work and concentrate, his relationships with other people, in short, to his healthy development. And while they can argue convincingly that if they had not separated, the years of living in a home with tension and conflict might have caused more serious emotional wounds to their children, most know that custody must, nevertheless, be handled carefully.

The more parents know about the effects on children of common accompaniments to custody matters—such things as parental fighting, custody disputes, cutting a child off from a parent, financial insecurity, separating siblings from one another, moving, the emotional problems which parents themselves go through as a result of divorce, and parents' dating and remarriage—the more effective they can be in helping their children.

Because separation and divorce are better understood, more common, and freer of stigma than they were fifty, fifteen, or even five years ago, they are perhaps a bit less trying for the children and adults who must go through them. Most children whose parents break up today have friends in the same position. But it has by no means become easy for the child of divorce. His teachers, parents of his friends, his peers still may be uncomfortable with divorce—perhaps with what they view as the incompleteness of single-parent families—and may tend to ignore the fact that it happened or let it be known in subtle ways that it is an undesirable way to live. Consequently the child of divorced parents still may feel the sting of being the outsider.

Beyond that, at any time in the past or present, every child of divorce has had to deal alone with his own personal demons—feeling scared, abandoned, lonely, angry, depressed, confused about the future.

The Real Challenge to Parents

As we have seen, during the past one hundred years children's rights began, struggled, and have survived to the point that today they come before those of mothers or fathers and each custody case is judged subjectively according to what is best for the child. Who is the child closest to? Who is the more suitable parent? Who will provide the better environment for the child? These are some of the key questions asked.

Deciding on a fair custody arrangement is one step in helping a child adjust to his parents' breakup. In this respect, lawmakers and judges have become more sensitive to and better informed about custody, though the system must continue to become more efficient. However, the greater challenge of custody, and the one that never stops, is going on to raise the children and establish a healthy family life for them after the separation, after the custody agreement, and after the divorce.

Custody is, in a sense, easier today than it was in former years when being part of a divorced family was strange and somewhat suspect. It is more difficult as well. Women's roles have changed radically. Women compete successfully in most formerly male-dominated pursuits, yet studies show they still have the major responsibility for the home and children. Men, too, are seeing their roles redefined and traditions changing daily. Add to this the pressures and confusions which face parents who live alone with their children or those who visit by appointment and it is understandable that they often feel torn and uncertain.

But there is one certainty. We, as parents, love and have the responsibility for our children. They love us and need us, married or divorced.

Chapter Three

WHAT IS CUSTODY?

Who will take Jimmy to the pediatrician? Should he go to Sunday School? What about a speech teacher for his lisp? Who will pay for summer camp? Where will he go for his birthday? Should he take music lessons? Is his friend Alec a bad influence? How much television should he watch?

The Essence

Normally, these responsibilities and decisions are part of the daily lives of two parents. However, where there is no longer a two-parent home, they are assigned to one or the other parent and become part of what is meant by having custody. Essentially, custody means being the primary caretaker and authority in a child's life. It involves having him physically around for the majority of the time, as well as providing him with food and clothing, deciding what type of education he will have, and seeing to it that he has appropriate opportunities to make and meet friends.

On a more emotional level, it involves caring—caring enough to give a child standards; to provide structure; to demand reasonable and consistent discipline; to make him feel loved and wanted and not there by sufferance; to allow him to express his aggression and help him learn to control it; and to involve oneself in his life. Caring, too, may mean putting a child's interests above one's own needs, including, in some instances, accepting a custody arrangement one did not wish for or living up to a visitation agreement only because it is best for a *child*'s emotional well-being.

Mary and Bert had been married ten years when they decided to separate. Six-year-old Alexandra was their only child. Mary worked as a fabric designer in an office six blocks from their apartment in downtown Atlanta, while Bert's job as a producer for a local television station included irregular working hours and frequent out-of-town business trips. Bert had always been very much involved with his daughter and after the separation was distraught at the thought of seeing her only once or twice a week. He disapproved of his wife's marijuana smoking and her occasional "oddball" parties with her artist friends. He decided to talk to his lawyer about suing for custody.

"Does she give the stuff to your daughter to smoke or even smoke it in front of her?" his lawyer asked Bert.

"Well no," Bert answered.

"Does she neglect or abuse the child?"

"No, certainly not."

"You see," the lawyer explained, "the thing is, Bert,

48

Mary works from nine to five, she has a good house-keeper there when Alex gets home from school and the truth is she's a damn good mother who's at home on most nights and when she's out the child is well taken care of.

"And look at you, Bert," he went on. "Some nights you work until ten. You're out of town every other week. The child wouldn't see you enough. I don't think you have much of a case."

After thinking it over, Bert agreed to Mary having custody providing he could spend most weekends with his daughter.

The Arrangements

There are various custody arrangements: "exclusive," "joint," "sole," "divided," "one-parent," "split," and "shared" are some of the terms used to describe those arrangements. When any custody provision is discussed, the terms should be clearly defined because such labels as joint or split custody are often used interchangeably or are misunderstood.

One-Parent Custody

One parent (sole or exclusive) custody is the most commonly used arrangement and it means most impor-tantly that either the mother, which is the usual case, or the father cares for the child on a daily basis and assumes responsibility for most of the child's needs.

The noncustodial parent usually sees the child accord-ing to a prescribed yet generally somewhat flexible sched-ule negotiated as part of the custody settlement.

Kurt and Maria separated with Maria taking sole

custody of nine-year-old Kim and eleven-year-old Nils. On alternate weekends Kurt picked up the children Friday afternoons and returned them Sunday evening. He kept them for a month in the summer until they were old enough to work, at which point they stayed at their mother's house during the week.

Joint Custody

In joint custody, sometimes called co- or shared custody, two parents share responsibility and authority over a child. It is a plan chosen by a small but growing number of parents and can work in several different ways. For example, in a joint-custody plan children can move back and forth between parents' homes or parents can move in and out of the main house. The children's time can also be handled in various ways. Some parents alternate half weeks while others exchange the children every week, month, or half year. Still other parents are less literal about their living patterns, and they agree, for example, that it would be best for the children's school schedule for them to live with one parent on weekdays and with the other parent on weekends.

The Robertsons ran their joint-custody arrangement in a typical manner. Billy and Matt lived in their mother's house and in their father's apartment on alternating weeks, making the change on Sunday evening.

Split or Divided Custody

Split (divided) custody means separated children. One or more children live with one parent and the other(s) with the other parent. This is not a commonly used arrangement and is generally found where there are special circumstances such as in the case of Nadine and Tom, where Tom, who worked for an oil company, was frequently transferred to different South American countries for stays of six months to a year at a time in each place. His fourteen-year-old son, Anthony, felt he would rather go with his father than not see him for such long stretches of time. Anthony visited his mother, who stayed in Texas with his nine-year-old sister, Christine, whenever his dad returned to the States.

Each type of custody has advantages and drawbacks for children as well as parents. These are discussed in detail in the following chapters.

PART TWO

CHOOSING THE RIGHT CUSTODY ARRANGEMENT

Chapter Four

PRIORITIES TO KEEP IN MIND IN WORKING OUT A CUSTODY ARRANGEMENT

True or False:

—Children believe the parent they are not living with doesn't want them.

—Joint custody makes children feel they don't belong anywhere.

—Boys should live with their fathers, girls with their mothers.

—Parents always put their children's interests first.

—Children should make their own decisions about custody.

—Split custody is the fairest arrangement for parents.

—Natural parents are always preferable to step- or foster parents.

—The type of custody arrangement is the main

factor in determining how a child will adjust to the parents' separation.

—Split custody is always a mistake.

—Young children are not much affected by parental divorce.

Studies have shown that none of the above is entirely true. Most of these commonly held ideas, however, probably do contain some truth. Even the experts disagree at times. Yet, after we talked with many divorced parents and professionals who work with families of divorce, it seems that finding the right custody arrangement is less complex than many people realize. The difficulty in making custody decisions often arises because at the highly emotional time at which parents must make these important decisions they may not be thinking clearly.

Psychologists often advise people who are under severe stress to avoid making major decisions until they are more settled emotionally. But newly separated parents, although under much stress, can't delay urgent decisions regarding their children, especially what the custody arrangement for the children is to be. Under the circumstances it is no wonder parents sometimes make mistakes.

"I was feeling so much guilt when I told Jerry I wanted a separation," recalls one woman "that I couldn't think straight. I even offered him custody of Adam because I was the one who wanted out. Sure, you tell yourself that you count too, that you've been unhappy all these years, that you should do something for yourself. But when it comes down to it you feel so guilty about breaking up the family."

Some parents subordinate their child's welfare to their own anger over a separation they didn't want. One woman who had several extramarital affairs and had never spent much time with her four-year-old son was nevertheless infuriated when her husband told her he wanted her out and that the boy would stay with him.

"Now every time she sees him," the father explained later, "my son comes home and tells me something like 'Daddy, Mommy says she loves me and wants to live with us but you made her go away. Why did you do that?'

"The child was terribly confused and angry at me until I told him some details about what had happened," the father went on. "I told Nicky his mother had hurt me a great deal and that you don't treat someone like that if you love them. He seems to understand a little better now, but who knows what she'll say to him next. Just last time Nicky arrived home he said, 'I told Mommy that even if she couldn't come here and sleep in your room she could sleep over with me.' "

Indeed, parents can do strange, surprising, sometimes damaging things to their children, including putting their own interests ahead of their children's at a time when the children are so vulnerable. Because the intense stress of separation and divorce can sometimes cause parents to act irrationally, many have said that being reminded of certain priorities might have prevented some of the errors they made in working out a custody arrangement for their children. The following points are considered by most professionals and by divorced parents as being the most important ones to keep in mind.

Step One: Choosing the Right Arrangement for Your Child

Choose the best possible custody arrangement for your child or children that is also reasonably well suited to your needs. This is not complicated or technical to work out. Will one of you have more time for the child than the other? Does he or she have special physical, educational, or emotional needs which one of you is better prepared to handle? Is he or she much closer to one of you than to the other? Are you more or less equally close to the child? What arrangement would cause the least disruption in his life? Can you cooperate with one another when it comes to your child? Can you separate your interests from your child's? Do you realize the importance of your child staying close to both parents?

There is no mystery or formula to choosing the custody arrangement that is best for your child. He will need as much love, attention, stability, and continuity as possible.

With the numerous cross pressures and tension of separation, some parents may not realize how important it is to give first priority in a custody decision to what is best for a child. Upset by their own stress, parents may compound children's suffering by refusing to cooperate in settling custody, and in some instances, with a bitter court struggle. This leads us to the next important point to remember.

Step Two: Try to Stay Out of Court

If at all possible try to stay out of court. Judges, attorneys, and psychiatrists repeatedly advise that mothers and fathers should make every effort to reach a custody agreement out of court. "Parents know their children better than anyone else. They know what's good for them and they can make the best decision provided they stick to the criterion of what's really best for the child," explained one psychiatrist.

"But I've seen contested custody cases that are selfish exercises on the part of one of the parents," explains a Houston judge. "Some parents hope to relieve their guilt about the divorce by saying they want custody when they actually don't. Others look for revenge on their ex-spouses for not giving them enough money or not letting them see the children enough, and they're not about to cooperate on anything."

There is also the occasional man or woman who does not want a separation. He or she is still in love with a spouse and will start a court proceeding over custody simply as a way of getting to see that person.

Conscious of their improved chances at winning custody, increased numbers of fathers are using the courts for reasons other than the children's well-being, according to judges and attorneys. "I have seen numerous cases of parents, usually but not always the father, who eventually offered to end the battle if their former spouses agree to change the financial or visitation arrangements," explained a leading New York matrimonial lawyer. "Other parents will never actually go to court but dangle it as a threat when the details of an agreement don't suit them. They don't necessarily want custody, but they use their right to custody as a bargaining device."

Dr. Albert Solnit of the Yale Child Study Center talks about couples who use litigation in order to stay attached. "They are long-time fighting pals," he says, and "although they can give up the love or the sexual aspects of their marriage they can't part with the fighting outlet."

Some parents find it difficult or impossible to work out a custody agreement together. Others report that consulting with a psychiatrist or psychologist, clergyman, social worker, or lawyer who specializes in custody work has helped them reach successful custody agreements

with a minimum of distress, conflict, or anger. Conciliation courts, discussed in greater detail in Chapter Seventeen, provide the services of psychologists and social
workers and have had a high rate of success in helping
parents settle cases that would otherwise have ended up
in courts. In the many states and counties without
conciliation courts, parents must seek out professional
advice on their own with the help perhaps of family
doctors or local mental health agencies. But an effective
consultant in a custody matter is worth the time and
expense.

Step Three: Move Quickly

Almost as important as arriving at a custody arrangement that is sound for your child is to get on with all the
changes accompanying the separation and custody plan
and let your child proceed with his own life. Set up
whatever new living arrangements there will be. Start the
visitation schedule. (Ideally there should never have been
an interruption in the child's relationship with either
parent.) If your child will have to change schools, try to
arrange for the change to begin either in September or
following Christmas vacation. And by all means keep the
changes in your child's life to a minimum. Remember,
familiar people, places, and routines are all helpful to
your child in coping with the major changes caused by
divorce and in withstanding the stress.

More than almost anything a child needs continuity in
his life if he is to develop his personality and abilities. A
long period of uncertainty before a child knows who he
will be living with, where his home will be, and how
often he will see his other parent, punctuated by argu-

ments, threats, and lawsuits can seriously disturb a child, interrupt his development, and make it hard for him to get on the right track again.

While children can get over an acute emotional shock, studies show that one of the greatest risks of custody and divorce is that it can become an extended trauma which keeps a child hanging emotionally and suspends his development. Michigan child psychiatrist Elissa Benedek and attorney Richard Benedek, who have collaborated on custody work and research, feel so strongly about this that they say a delay in resolving custody is more likely to be harmful to a child than a prompt decision based on imperfect knowledge.

Step Four: End the Conflict

Another crucial step which can help your child make the transition from the two-parent family to life with one parent is to end the conflict between you and your spouse as quickly as possible. It is likely that when you separated you told your child that there was too much fighting, and that he would be better off in a calm atmosphere. But, if he is regularly upset by parents arguing at the door or on the telephone, there will be as much tension in the home as before the separation. A child under this kind of continuing stress at home stands a good chance of being too distracted to work well in school, to make friends, or to mature in a healthy way. Should the stress continue for more than a matter of weeks, a child's school and social life may suffer permanent setbacks.

Is your custody plan in your child's best interests? Did you act promptly and not extend his or her trauma? Has the conflict between you and your spouse subsided to a point that it does not interfere with your child's daily life?

If so, your custody decision should not leave your child with major problems. If not, you are not alone but you have important work to do.

In theory no custody arrangement in and of itself can determine how a child of divorce will adjust. Yet because many factors crucial to the success of a custody arrangement vary from parent to parent— lifestyle, work schedule, free time, income, place of residence, ability to handle special problems or needs of the child, tolerance for a life with children—one arrangement may be decidedly better for a particular family than another would be. Where parents honestly choose the arrangement most realistic for them, their children stand the best chance at a healthy adjustment.

Chapter Five

ONE-PARENT CUSTODY (Pros and Cons)

"It can seem overwhelming at first. I'd never cooked any big-time meals and I'd never cleaned house except for emptying an ash tray occasionally, and I'd certainly never had to cuff a pair of pants for a five-year-old. Most important of all, I'd never had to do all these things all the time," is the way one father, who as a married man had shared in the cooking, dishwashing, and marketing, explained having full custody of his two children.

A mother with full custody and most of the financial responsibility for her two children explained, "In my situation I have to be the parent, the homemaker, and the breadwinner. At the end of every day I'm physically and emotionally exhausted." Also concerned about not giving the children enough time because of her heavy schedule, she confesses, "I'm confused a good deal of the time. I ask myself 'Am I doing the right thing? Am I doing enough?' "

What Is It?

One-parent custody, also referred to as "exclusive" or "sole" custody, is the arrangement on which more divorced parents settle than on any other. It is the form of custody that professionals such as Albert Solnit, Anna Freud, New York State Chief Justice Charles Breitel, and many others favor.

In exclusive custody, one parent, usually the mother, has the children in her care for the majority of the time. In almost all cases the other parent has regular visitation time, usually for one or two days each week. Where the mother has custody the father usually pays child support, but with more mothers working, fewer fathers carry the full financial responsibility. Mothers seldom pay significant child support where their former husbands have custody, although this is changing too. An exclusive custody arrangement or any other arrangement may be changed if there is a significant change in the emotional or marital circumstances of one of the parents. But this may involve going to court.

The majority of divorced parents find one-parent custody to be the most workable arrangement. But virtually everyone will tell you that it takes hard work and dedication.

How Do Children Feel About One-Parent Custody?

While there will be occasional problems and a great deal of work, one-parent custody offers a child what many authorities feel is essential for him—one primary parent who can make important decisions regarding his life, one primary home, his room, his toys, his favorite blanket. While these children no longer see one of their parents as often as they had before, experts say they have what is most important: a consistent, predictable home life and the parent to whom they are close. In fact many children in joint-custody arrangements ended up asking to be with one parent on a full-time basis. One twelve-year-old boy explained, "How would you like living in one house in one part of town on Mondays, Tuesdays, and Wednesdays and in another house in another part of town on the other days. Sometimes I wake up at night and I don't know where I am."

For some families sole custody is the best choice by far. Where one parent is clearly the more responsible or loving or where a child has a special medical or emotional problem which can be handled better by one parent, this form of custody is the wisest choice. And where the wife or husband has done most of the child rearing and the other parent wants no additional involvement, it would be a mistake to force more responsibility on him. While he might accept it out of guilt, this would be very bad for the children. Of course, children who are over the age of ten or eleven should be consulted.

Psychiatrist Dr. Alan Levy cautions parents to remember that one-parent custody is a lopsided arrangement and that they should find ways "to shore up the lack." Arranging for your child to spend time with adults, such as teachers and good friends who are the same sex as your former spouse, can help to correct the imbalance. Encourage frequent and easy contact between your children and their other parent. It's good for their self-esteem to have two parents who care and are still involved.

See Chapter Ten for a more detailed discussion of possible psychological problems of children in this and other custody arrangements.

How Do Parents Feel About It?

Keeping the house clean, cooking, disciplining, never seeming to have enough money, time or peace and quiet to be able to get things done the way they should be, having whatever romantic moments you're lucky enough to enjoy inevitably interrupted, listening to play by play accounts of soccer games, seeing to it that the children remember their lunches and do their book reports, buying their clothes, teaching them to keep their rooms neat, screening their friends, listening to their bad dreams, comforting them while the dentist does root-canal work, monitoring their TV watching, breaking up arguments, playing Monopoly, running a pick-up and delivery service to music, swimming or other lessons, playing Santa Claus and the tooth fairy, going to P.T.A. meetings and reading books and articles on how to talk to children, what to feed them, what methods they should be using to learn to read, are hard enough when two people are sharing the work. But when one person has all the jobs and may earn some or all of the family income as well, it is understandable that he or she can feel physically over-worked and emotionally overwhelmed.

Mother or Father Custody? Life Without Mother, Life Without Father

More women are pursuing ambitions beyond home and children and entrusting their children to housekeepers and baby-sitters. And increasing numbers of men are revealing their nurturing abilities and asserting what they feel is their equal right to custody. Because most families choose a one-parent custody arrangement, many people are curious and some are concerned about which parent really is better for the children. Among professionals there is some difference of opinion as to which parent for which sex at which age is preferable.

Andrew S. Watson, Professor of Law and Psychiatry at the University of Michigan, holds what still seems to be the majority opinion. He feels that children are best off with their mothers when they are below the teen-age years, "provided the mother is emotionally capable." In adolescence Watson says, "The like-sexed parent becomes more important since learning to become male or female is the principal psychological task for that age group."

"Mothers tend to be better with very young children— infants and toddlers," says child psychiatrist Richard Gardner, who feels that as children get older parents become more equal in their ability to do the job.

As father custody becomes more common, psychologists and sociologists are studying it more carefully and finding out that many fathers are highly motivated and able to be full-time parents. In a study headed by Dennis

K. Orthner at the University of North Carolina in Greensboro on single-parent fatherhood, the researcher's conclusion was, "These fathers feel quite capable and successful in their ability to be the primary parents of their children. The confidence they express and the satisfaction they seem to derive in fatherhood is very difficult to deny."

The one out of ten fathers who assumes custody today is, according to recent research, generally an involved, loving parent, and while some custodial fathers worry that they are not measuring up in some way, in actuality they do quite well.

More important than who should have custody, however, may be the effects on a child of being deprived of the parent who does not have custody. This deprivation of course does not apply to all children but only to those who have one parent who loses close touch with them. Because numerous studies on children who live with one parent suggest possible lifelong effects which being cut off from a parent can have, we should be just as concerned about the effect of a parent being "absent" as we are about which parent has custody.

An important effect has been that children whose parents were divorced when the children were under eight years of age frequently were depressed in later life to the point that depression became their almost automatic reaction to all forms of stress.

Since mothers have custody in roughly 90 percent of single-parent homes, most research has looked into the effects on children of "father absence." Years from now there may be as much information on children growing up without full-time mothers.

An extra parent in the home is an insurance policy. Someone who is there if the other parent is ill, busy, tired, or emotionally unavailable. Beyond that, while mothers and fathers share in child-rearing responsibilities and do many of the *same* things for children, the skills, values, the ideas which they tend to emphasize are usually *different*, and children are enriched by the influence of both.

At the risk of sounding sexist, it still seems to be true that the average mother is the more accepting, more understanding parent, while the typical father demands more discipline, is more concerned with his child's ambitions and future place in life, and thinks more about his child's identification with his or her sex role.

In Robert Frost's words, "You don't have to deserve your mother's love. You have to deserve your father's. He's more particular. One's a Republican, one's a Democrat. The father is always a Republican towards his son and his mother's always a Democrat."

Not having a parent around on a regular basis affects boys and girls differently. Research has shown that boys with fathers at home or closely involved with them handle their lives and their aggression more constructively, whereas boys without fathers available are more likely to lose their direction—to underachieve in school and often to get into trouble—with teachers, the police, or other authority figures. A boy whose father is not around on a regular basis does not have someone to model himself after or "identify with." Many such boys feel their fathers abandoned them and may come to distrust men. At the same time they can become surrounded by and too dependent on women. Some boys in this position attempt to camouflage their dependence on women with a veneer of "masculine" toughness.

Girls react differently. At first, not having a father around may appear to have little effect on them. Psychologists explain that a girl without a father at home often will not show obvious signs of her loss until she has passed puberty. A common result of being without a father is that she will not trust men, may not feel comfortable or relaxed with them, and consequently will not have much chance at successful relationships with men. In adolescence and adult life this often shows up in extreme attention-getting behavior around men and, at times, promiscuity. The other side of the coin is the girl who later in life may be unusually inhibited around men or avoid them entirely.

Many children of divorce continue to have a good deal of love and attention from two parents. But for those not as fortunate, it is fair to conclude that a good number of girls and boys, who grow up without having one of their parents around regularly, feel some degree of abandonment, have more difficulty in relating to the opposite sex, and are more likely than other children to have marital problems.

The other side of the coin is the full-time single parent whose ex-spouse is not regularly involved with the children. He or she will have a much harder job than other parents.

While children growing up with one parent are *disadvantaged* (they don't have the advantage of two devoted parents and they will inevitably feel some of the anger, guilt, low self-esteem, depression, or rebelliousness which touch most children of divorce), they don't necessarily have to be *deprived*—of love, involvement, structure, affection, discipline, emotional support, and all the factors that figure into a person's emotional health and well-being. The hitch is that one parent with whatever supporting figures he or she can find, must provide for all the child's needs.

Easily said, not as easily done. It will mean being on constant call—physically and emotionally—encouraging children to talk about how they feel and why they feel as they do, reassuring them that an uninvolved parent is behaving as he is because of the problems within himself, including children in activities and relationships with new people, particularly with adults of the same sex of their "absent" parent, and by caring and being willing to help them with their problems.

But as one mother said, "When you try your best the children know that. Love goes a long way."

The Noncustodial Parent

In most cases where there is a custodial parent, there is usually a visiting parent who spends roughly a day or two each week with the children, keeps in touch with them on other days, and contributes financially to their support. The parent must schedule appointments to see his children, is not in control of major decisions regarding them, and often worries that his children will move away or that he will be replaced by a new lover or spouse in their other parent's life.

Yet, what seems to make so many parents most comfortable with the one-parent arrangement, aside from the clear delineation of authority which it offers and the fact that it is probably the most stable setup, is that it affords the noncustodial parent the opportunity to work at a career without the distraction of children at home to cook for, do laundry for, help with homework, and be there to hear the endless stream of minor and major problems.

Many noncustodial parents report that they have a full

relationship with their children, seeing them several times a week and talking with them on the telephone frequently. Others see their children less often but don't lose touch. "It's so good to have that shred of family life even if it's only one day a week," said one father who had just been separated.

For a more detailed discussion of part-time parents see Chapter Eleven.

Problems of One-Parent Custody

1. The Physical Burden

"When one of my children isn't doing well in school they call me. When they need a troop leader they call me. If one of them gets sick at camp, I pick him up. If the younger one has a fever, I can't leave her alone, so I keep the other one home from school. I drive to after-school activities. I wanted to look for a full-time job but I couldn't work and handle two kids properly," exclaims one frustrated mother. "You have friends you can call on, sure," she continued. "But not *too* often."

Certainly friends will help out when they can, but use them sparingly and give something in return. If you have a friend who takes your child to school whenever the other one is sick, offer to do the same for her. Where you can't reciprocate in the same way, do something special like having all the children of your helpful friends over for a barbecue or a costume party.

2. Trying to Do Everything

"I find trying to be mother *and* father is the hardest part," said another mother. Psychiatrists and psychologists have said that aside from having most of the responsibility, parents with sole custody find that a big strain is having to walk the fine line between being too accepting and too demanding—between being able to be a disciplinarian when necessary and a warm, loving parent. This problem is expressed by mothers as well as fathers, each emphasizing different concerns. Many mothers say they have more difficulty exercising the necessary discipline and control while more fathers feel that whatever inadequacies they have as full-time parents are more in the area of giving affection, nurture, and dealing with children's sometimes unpredictable emotions—most especially temper tantrums in young children and moodiness in older children.

3. Organization

Diane echoed the sentiments of many parents with custody. "Getting *organized* was my biggest stumbling block. I work from nine to five. Making breakfasts, packing lunches, making the beds, getting myself ready for work in the morning and then marketing, cooking, play dates for the kids, homework, baths, and sometimes laundry at night had me frazzled for a while," she said.

Dan, a working father with full-time custody of his six-year-old son, also mentioned the importance of getting into routines. He made the observation that organization is not only helpful to the parent but crucial to a child. "My son is much happier with a lot of regularity and routine," he said. "It makes his life easier if he knows what's going on—who picks him up from school, when he eats dinner, when he goes to bed, knowing that he'll go to school on time each day and won't be overtired. It's terribly important and helps him to function better."

4. Being a Main Source of Comfort

Where a child is having emotional difficulties following a separation, and most children do have rough spots, this

73

too falls on the shoulder of the custodial parent to handle. ("Besides the day to day cooking, dishes, laundry, and that kind of thing, I have to deal with the fact that my children's mother *left*—walked out!" one father told me. "One of my sons, the five-year-old, was extremely upset about not seeing his mother, he was feeling worthless, acting up in school, hitting other kids, couldn't sleep. One night around the time of his birthday and his mother's birthday, which fall two days apart, he had had such a tantrum that he actually tore out clumps of his hair! I think he scared himself at that point and decided to listen to me a bit more. After a lot of work—getting him to talk, cry, punch pillows, generally getting things off his chest—I think we've turned a corner," this father went on. "But it takes constant time and effort."

5. Being Alone in a World of Children

Being alone in a world of children makes the job harder according to many parents. "Without any input from a spouse, you sometimes feel that you can't get back what you put in. You feel you need someone to put your arms around at the end of the day," is the way Dan described his situation.

"As for a social life, who has the time for a regular social life? Baby-sitters are expensive and sometimes they are reluctant to work for you if you're a man."

Many parents with custody reject the likely social outlet of single-parent groups as being, in one mother's words, "Made up of too many predatory types or those looking for a shoulder to cry on." Others have found them to be therapeutic in that they bring them together with people in situations similar to their own and provide other adults for their children to meet. Because single-parent groups vary widely, they are in most cases worth looking into.

Not only is it often lonely to have sole custody but as Dan explained it, "Other people hardly understand a parent's position of having to work full-time and have full responsibility for a home and children. With nonworking mothers, people expect them to be home and don't realize that it's even harder if you have to be the sole support and a full-time homemaker and parent," he went on. "If other people are single, they're busy with work and dates. They lead a more spontaneous life which you can't join in if you have children at home. And my married friends take their kids pretty much in stride. Everything is just more of a hassle for a working, single parent."

Divorced mothers who are at home full-time with their children, on the other hand, sometimes wish they had more outside stimulation. "Conversations with a five- and a nine-year-old are fine," said one mother, "but there are so many times when I'd like to have an *adult* to talk with."

"Loneliness is a tremendous problem for men and women with custody," according to child psychiatrist Dr. Andre Derdeyn. "No matter how bad a marriage is, your life is shaped by the person you live with."

Once that person is gone, so is a good deal of the structure of your life. Being a wife or husband, a companion, a sex partner, part of a couple at social activities are anchors one holds on to. As they slip away and are not easily replaced, a person can be left feeling temporarily unstable, without a footing, without boundaries. This happens most often to women who had spent most of their time taking care of the home and family. These women may be the most prone to falling into the traps of one-parent custody which will be discussed in the next section.

Traps of One-Parent Custody

During this decidedly vulnerable period, for your own and your children's sake, try to guard against three deadly traps of one-parent custody.

First, many custodial parents become so depressed that they are slowed down to the point of rarely going out of their houses, seeing few people, and pursuing few interests. If this happens to you, your children—who need you to provide *extra* structure, contact with *new* people, and *more* activity—may become seriously depressed themselves.

Talk sessions and exchanges of ideas with psychiatrists or psychologists, family counselors, clergymen experienced in family problems, or groups such as Parents Without Partners have helped many newly separated parents talk about feelings such as grief and anger getting in their way (to "process their losses" as psychiatrists say) and have helped them start doing things to get them out of their depression (Part Five discusses sources of professional help).

"Just finding out that other people had some of the same feelings I did made me stronger," said one woman about the weekly meeting of single parents and counselors which she attends. "And we have Saturday afternoon activities with the children, like baseball games, ice skating, and hikes," she added. "It's been very good for my son because there are men and women in the group."

If you don't do something about that slowed-down depressed feeling, the *second* danger to your children is that you will come to rely too much on them and in so doing will catapult them beyond their years and their ability to cope.

Pauline didn't realize that she was crossing some of the unspoken but very definite and necessary boundaries between a parent and a child. After her separation she began sleeping in the same room as her twelve-year-old daughter, revealing sexual concerns to her, confiding her financial worries to her daughter and her fourteen-year-old son, Charlie, and often asking them to stay at home with her instead of going out with their friends. On the few occasions when she attended parties, she brought Charlie along as her escort.

Pauline's daughter Jane, who had always been an excellent student, began getting into trouble for truancy. Pauline met with the principal and some of Jane's teachers who said they had noticed that the girl seemed worried and distracted lately. They asked Pauline if things had changed in any way at home. Pauline explained that she had recently separated from her husband and that she was depending on her daughter and son for a great deal of emotional support.

At the principal's suggestion, Pauline and Jane met with the school psychologist. Pauline was helped to see that she had been demanding too much of her children, especially Jane, and getting too close to them in inappropriate ways. After several meetings with the psychologist, Jane's situation has improved and Pauline has asked for a recommendation of an outside therapist that she could see on a continuing basis in order to work through some of her anxieties over the separation.

The *third* emotional danger to your child can occur if you continue to be so angry at your former spouse or so depressed for a long period of time that you poison your child's relationship with his other parent. If the child hears his other parent maligned and criticized week after week, month after month, eventually he may adopt the same negative opinion and not be able to have a normal relationship with him. Where the war goes on between parents, a child can't help but feel guilty, helpless (things were supposed to get better but they're not) and angry. He needs the best possible relationship with his other parent or he simply will not be able to function as well as he could.

One-Parent Custody Becomes More Manageable

The thought of taking on full custody is often frightening to parents at first, but many say while it is hard work they find that after an adjustment period, which admittedly can take a year or more, many of the physical and organizational pressures begin to ease.

"For awhile I felt like I was on a race track," Diane explained. "I was working and taking care of the children and the house. After about a year I made some changes. Now I don't expect as much of myself. One night a week we get a pizza and another we go out for hamburgers. The girls now take care of their own rooms—sort of. I had to decide what was really important and what wasn't. Now I'm amazed at how well our routines work," she said.

"And some of the problems you had in the beginning seem to fade as the children get older. The kids help you and each other more than a lot of children do who live with two parents," commented a mother with two sons and a daughter. "After a while they realize that we're all in this together and everyone pitches in. It's made my children more responsible."

Dan explained that even for a father who works full time, has full custody of his child, and a former wife who is unavailable, things have gotten better and he is emotionally more settled. "I've been seeing a woman for several months now. She's divorced with three children who get along well with my son. They're having a fine time. We'll see where the future leads."

Because finances are usually spread thin after divorce, some single parents ease their financial responsibilities by taking in a boarder, often a student, to contribute to the rent and sometimes the baby-sitting or housework. Others decide to share a house with someone in the same situation as they.

Should Separated and Divorced Parents Live Near One Another?

Parents with custody as well as the psychiatrists, psychologists, social workers, and judges who counsel them agree on the importance of *both* parents remaining involved with their children after a separation. "It is most crucial to the children that one parent doesn't drop out of their lives," says Dr. Gardner. Can parents therefore live more than a short drive or bus trip apart?

The ideal custody arrangement allows a child easy access to both parents. Proximity is a factor to consider in providing that access. But how important is it? Important enough to sacrifice a job opportunity or a relationship with someone you love?

There are those parents who become too single-minded about staying physically close to their children. Often their guilt stands in the way of their common sense, forcing them to make unreasonable sacrifices.

Katherine had returned to law school after she and Mark were divorced. Because their two children, Christopher, nine, and Peter, seven, were in school all day,

Katherine had managed to carry full-credit loads, completing her law training in exactly three years.

Searching for a job in the New York metropolitan area turned up no offers for a novice attorney. On the advice of a friend, Katherine applied for positions in the southwestern United States. She had heard there wasn't the same surplus of lawyers that she faced in the East.

Two offers came through, one in San Diego, the other in Phoenix. Katherine decided to grab the opportunity, take the boys, and head west to southern California.

Mark did not want to lose his relationship with his children, yet he couldn't, in fairness, try to stop Katherine from accepting her job offer. (Even where divorce agreements stipulate in writing that the custodial parent cannot move beyond a certain distance, usually fifty miles, this point can usually be superseded for health or employment reasons.)

Mark was distraught. He knew the separation would be bad for him and he felt it wouldn't be good for the children either. He contemplated moving.

He was forty-five years old and still with the same insurance company he had joined eighteen years earlier. There had been college, three years in the Navy, two years as a teacher, and the insurance business. He was now vice-president, one of twelve, and felt he was well regarded both within his company and in the business. But, moving now would mean giving up some of the benefits he had worked hard for. It would also mean leaving his eighty-year-old mother, who was in a nursing home with no other relatives nearby.

After talking it over with Katherine and with friends, Mark decided to risk moving and finding a job in California. He figured he could carry himself for at least a year if a job didn't come through, and with Katherine working he didn't have to worry as much for the time being about child support.

Having lined up interviews, Mark left the security of being highly positioned in a large successful firm along with the familiarity with the part of the country where he had spent his life.

He says today that he never regretted his choice. "I'm as close to the boys as ever and even if I hadn't been lucky enough to find the kind of job I wanted relatively quickly, I feel I would have lost a lot more by being three thousand miles away. I think the boys like it too that I was willing to move to be near them," said Mark. "We feel bad about my mother though. But I'm going to be able to get to New York on business from time to time and can visit her then. I think I'll even take the boys there this summer. She'd like that."

Hank's was a different case. He was a former advertising manager for a Milwaukee-based magazine and had been divorced for a year and a half and unemployed for three months. His former wife worked as a secretary. With Hank's income cut off and their savings shrinking fast, she and the children were becoming financially strapped while Hank's creeping depression kept him inside his apartment in front of the television more and more of the time.

One morning he received a telephone call from the vice-president of marketing of an electronics firm he had interviewed with. Mr. Schmidt asked him to come back for a second interview. "The opening," he said "will be in our St. Louis branch. We think you might be the man for the job and it would be a big step up for you."

"St. Louis?" Hank asked. "I see . . . listen, let me get

back to you. I'll have to think about it. It's a long distance you know and I have children to think of."

Hank decided against the second interview and the likelihood of an excellent job. He continued to look for work in Milwaukee, feeling progressively worse, until six months later he was forced to take the same job that had helped him work his way through college—waiting on tables.

In Hank's case, although he meant well, he was not thinking clearly. His decision helped neither himself nor his children. "Other parts of our lives affect what we do with our children," says divorce researcher Dr. Stanley Cohen. "If our work and social lives are more satisfying by living *less* close to children, we may nevertheless be better parents for it because we're happier."

The key to custody success and children's well-being seems to be both parents wanting to stay involved with their children. This means keeping in touch with them and making it easy for them to keep in touch with you.

Give them your work and home telephone numbers. Communicate with them several times a week. If you live far enough away to make telephoning expensive, write letters to them and encourage them to do the same. Long interesting letters, sometimes including photographs, news clippings, or cartoons you think they would appreciate can be read over and over and give them tangible proof that you care. Many parents and children also mail cassettes taped with talk, singing, jokes and riddles.

Living near one's children is certainly a help in staying close to them and it facilitates spending enough time to keep the ties alive. At the same time living nearby doesn't guarantee a close relationship and living some distance away does not preclude it.

More important than the number of miles between children and parents, the deciding factor in the success of any custody plan is the parents' *attitude* toward their children. One father explained, "If you really care, if you're really committed, you won't allow anything to keep you from staying close to your kids."

"The rest," says U.C.L.A. psychiatrist Dr. Edward Ritvo, "is window dressing."

One-parent custody offers children and custodial parents a predictable, consistent arrangement. Both understand who is in charge. For the custodial parent this allows simpler decision making and makes potentially disruptive contact with a former spouse necessary on a less frequent basis than would be the case in a joint-custody arrangement. The children will not see their parent quite as much as they would in a more shared arrangement, but neither will there be as much chance of loyalty conflicts.

Your children's needs and feelings, your own and your spouse's wishes, and the relationship between you and the person you are no longer married to should determine whether this custody arrangement is right for your family.

Chapter Six

JOINT CUSTODY:
The Best of Both?

"Neither of us wanted the demands or responsibilities of full custody," explained Marguerite, a Detroit advertising copywriter who recently separated from her husband, Frank, an attorney. Each has the children three days a week, with grandmothers filling in on Wednesday afternoons at Marguerite's house. Neither feels overwhelmed as they might with full custody they say, nor do they feel out of touch as visiting parents often do.

What Is It?

Joint custody, sometimes called co-custody, shared custody, or co-parenting, an arrangement with several arguments in its favor, has developed a small but articulate following in recent years, particularly in some metropolitan areas.

In joint custody, separated or divorced parents agree to act as equal partners in raising the children. Both parents share in decisions regarding where the children live, where they go to school, who their friends are and in what activities they are involved. They share in paying the bills as equitably as their incomes allow, spend roughly the same amount of time with the children, and otherwise participate in all decisions and responsibilities having to do with them.

How Do Children Feel About Joint Custody?

I wondered whether Marguerite and Frank's children minded moving back and forth between their parents' homes.

"No," said seven-year-old Earl, "my dad and I do a lot of things together. We watch the basketball games on television on Thursday nights and as long as it's not real cold, we barbecue everything on his patio."

"I don't really mind," explained ten-year-old Amanda, "except that if I forget one of my books at the house on the day I'm going to Dad's, I have to call Mom and ask her to bring it over to my father's apartment and that makes her mad. But, even though I have to sleep on the living room couch at my dad's, I'm glad he wants us around and doesn't just come on Sundays like some kids' fathers do."

How Do Parents Feel About It?

"With this arrangement, the spontaneity between a parent and child doesn't have to end the way it can with one-parent custody," explained one father. Joint custody also may be less likely to leave a child feeling abandoned or rejected by either parent.

Many claim that it most closely approximates what the child had before the separation.

Joint custody has a feature most people don't mention. It leaves parents equal in the eyes of their children, not one a winner, the other a loser. Neither parent comes out appearing less able or less interested. No child wants to think his mother or father can't measure up, particularly as a parent.

"We're both still involved with the kids on a day-to-day basis," said Frank, "and we can cooperate when it comes to them. If their mother had them more this month than I did, we'll make up for it next month."

It sounded almost too ideal until Frank admitted that his children "can play me off against their mother," and said he feels that he buys too many toys and gives too many surprises like dinners at restaurants and movies to win the children's affections or, perhaps, in his mind, because he feels he must keep on a par with their mother. "Not her, though," he said about Marguerite with a trace of anger, "she's tough with the kids, and they're crazy about her."

While Marguerite's and Frank's situation has its subtle problems, one explanation for the arrangement working well may be that both parents wanted the separation and the joint-custody arrangement. Because there is less of the bitterness in this family than in those where one party is angry over the separation, the parents are able to talk to each other in a reasonable manner about the children. "We don't agree on everything," Marguerite quickly pointed out. "We still disagree about how much television they should watch, about the religious training they should have, and about some other things, but we're usually able to talk until we reach a compromise."

"One thing I think we're doing," Frank added, "and it's essential if joint custody is going to work, is that the children know that in my house they do things one way and in their mother's house they may do them a different way, but there'll be no talk of 'Mommy lets us do this . . .' In Daddy's house, Daddy makes the rules. In Mommy's house, Mommy makes the rules and that's that. Of course, my ex-wife and I try not to be too far apart on what the rules are."

The result of this amicable custody arrangement, which followed an unusually amicable separation, is that Earl and Amanda have continuing relationships with both of their parents and the children feel secure in the knowledge that both parents love them.

In today's world of working parents, joint custody can work especially well for families in which both parents have demanding jobs and neither feels comfortable with the responsibilities of full custody.

Joint Custody Can Be a Compromise

Sometimes, joint custody is agreed to as a compromise, the best solution a parent can hope for.

"I wanted to go to court and try to get custody of my daughter," explained one father. "My wife isn't unfit, but I didn't like the company she was keeping. Then I realized that a trial would be long and ugly and that there was a good chance I would lose anyway. I settled on joint custody and now I'll try to be the main influence in my daughter's life."

Problems of Joint Custody

Those who have found joint custody to be an un-satisfactory arrangement point out four basic reasons for their thinking:

1. One Parent Often Cannot Stay Sufficiently Involved

Bobby Colton's is a good example of a well-intentioned family who chooses joint custody because it sounds good but who, realistically, cannot handle it.

Their arrangement ran one way one week and worked in reverse during alternate weeks:

During *Week I*, Bobby spent four days, Sunday, Mon-day, Tuesday, and Wednesday with his mother. He spent Thursday, Friday, and Saturday with his father. On Sunday morning, between nine and ten, he walked the three blocks back to his mother's home.

During *Week II*, Bobby stayed at his mother's house only three days, Sunday, Monday, and Tuesday and went to his father's house a day earlier—after school on Wednesday. He stayed there until Sunday morning.

As with many working parents, there were meetings, emergencies, deadlines, and business trips which came up, particularly for Bobby's father. Soon the boy was spending more time with his dad's housekeeper than with his father. To make matters more confusing for him, his parents disagreed on the way Bobby should dress and had him wheel his clothes in a large red wagon when he walked back and forth between his father's apartment and his mother's house.

Finally, Bobby marshaled his courage and asked his father, "Dad, couldn't I just live in the house with Mom on school days and see you on my days off?" On Bobby's suggestion, the family changed their arrangement and found that the boy seemed happier.

2. A Transient Life?

Critics of joint custody point out the transient quality of situations like Bobby's. "A child doesn't feel he belongs anywhere when he has to shuttle back and forth constantly," says one psychiatrist.

Recognizing the difficulties involved in moving children around on a regular basis, some parents try a joint-custody solution as Jane and Leonard did. They leave their children in their original home and do the shuttling themselves, each one living in the house for one week and in an apartment on alternate weeks.

3. The Expense

While this sounds like an almost fairytale solution for children of divorce, it should be considered carefully. First, it is usually a more expensive arrangement than others. It means maintaining three residences, one main home for the children and the parent who is living in, and one for each parent on his off week. Where there are young children, this arrangement will require the services of a housekeeper in virtually every case because at least one parent will be working when the children arrive home from school, or have holidays or vacations. In the case of Jane and Leonard, while Jane did not work full-time, they needed to hire a full-time housekeeper to be with the children after school, on certain evenings, and occasionally overnight to accommodate Leonard's business schedule. (While they didn't need full-time help, they were forced to hire a full-time housekeeper because they found, as have many other families, that good part-time child-care is difficult, often impossible to find.) They had heard too many stories like the one about Thomas, whose mother came home one afternoon on a cold, rainy October day to find Thomas outside in the yard, unsupervised, playing in dungarees and a wet T-shirt. Their babysitter, a woman with an erratic job history who was the only person the parents could find who would work parttime, was inside talking on the telephone.

Furthermore, in many such arrangements, at least one of the parents does not have a real home. Leonard "lived" in his law office, which meant he kept his clothes in the office closet and slept on the couch. There were no kitchen or shower facilities. Leonard explained that having no real home made it harder for him to adjust to the separation. "I'm living out of a suitcase," he said.

In fact, any type of joint-custody arrangement tends to be more expensive than one-parent custody. Because each parent generally wants to provide a "real home" for the children who spend roughly half their time there, this means maintaining two relatively sizable homes. Some parents with joint custody argue, though, that this arrangement makes it more possible for the mother to work and increase the family income.

4. How Permanent Will It Be?

A year after her divorce, Jane faced what is probably the most important drawback which this arrangement has for children. She met a man whom she liked very much and decided to live with.

"Now that I'm living with Claude, we're going to have to change our custody situation," she said. While joint custody, where parents do the moving, appears to offer children the most stability, it may be setting them up for a major disappointment because it probably will not last long. In Jane's case, once she became involved with

Claude, her staying with the children for a week at a time would have been objectionable to him and bringing Claude into the house would probably not have been acceptable to Leonard.

Foreseeing this possibility, Jane and Leonard had included in their separation agreement a promise to move to other quarters if either became attached to a new partner. At this point, Leonard lives in the house on a full-time basis and has taken on full custody for the time being. Every other weekend, the children visit their mother in the new apartment she shares with Claude. The apartment is so small that none of them would be comfortable if the visits were longer.

What the Experts Say

Many professionals feel that not only this but *any* form of joint custody leaves children too uncertain. "It doesn't settle the battle," explains New York child psychologist Dr. Katherine Cobb. "If parents can't agree as married people, they usually can't agree after divorce on issues regarding their children, sometimes highly charged issues dealing with education, religion, friends, and money, and they'll just get into further arguments. She feels, as do many experts, that one parent should have the final say in these matters.

A family does not come to an end after a separation or divorce if there are children. Both parents continue to see the children and usually, to some degree, each other. Joint custody means that they must see each other more than with any other arrangement.

There is school to discuss and friends, vacation plans, behavior problems, extracurricular activities, medical and dental treatment, Christmas and birthday gifts, choices of movies, all the myriad details of children's lives. If one parent is still angry over the separation or what preceded it, the frequent contact necessary in joint custody may spark even more hostility and further upset the children. (See Chapter Ten for a discussion of psychological problems of children of divorce.)

Billy's case is an example of the resentment which some children are exposed to following a separation or divorce and of the trap of being "caught in the middle." It is one kind of situation where joint custody is not appropriate and may be the worst possible outcome for a child.

One afternoon as they passed a shoe store, Billy said to his mother, "Hey, Mom, look at those sneakers. Can I get a pair like that? Mine are too small."

"If your father weren't starving us, maybe I could buy you those. I practically have to buy cat food for us to eat," his mother answered.

That evening at McDonald's, the boy's father quizzed him about whether his mother had been going out at night, how late she came home, whether she talked on the telephone often and to whom. After a while, Billy stopped eating his dinner. When his father asked him what was wrong, the boy explained that he had a stomachache.

"Separated or divorced couples whose marriages live on in recriminations and suspicions could not manage a joint-custody arrangement and shouldn't attempt it," said one psychiatrist whose opinion is typical of many in the field.

Chief Judge Charles D. Breitel of the New York Court of Appeals, the highest court on the state level, and the other six members of that court, stated in June of 1978 that joint custody is inappropriate where parents are "persistently and severely embattled." As with any concept, what works for one family is not necessarily right for another.

Dr. Solnit has seen families where joint-custody arrangements, rather than being in the children's interests, were, in his opinion, "camouflages for staying married." Some parents opt for joint custody because they aren't ready to give up their relationship entirely. A joint-custody arrangement may even include legal veto power (written into the separation agreement) over new marriage or live-in partners in their ex-spouse's lives. "If a new mate is unacceptable to the other parent," says Solnit, "there can always be the threat of him saying, 'I don't think I want the children in that atmosphere or around that guy or whatever.' "

Are Judges Using Joint Custody to Avoid Difficult Decisions?

Professor Henry Foster, Chairman of the American Bar Association's Family Law section, sees joint custody decisions by judges as "something of a copout" to avoid difficult decisions or accusations of sex discrimination. Others feel that those judges who award custody to parents jointly are the most advanced in their thinking. They see it as a practical adaptation to the high divorce rate and a way of restructuring the family in order to give both parents a chance to continue being close to and involved with their children.

Jury Still Out

Joint custody is still too recent and limited a phenomenon to be evaluated conclusively. It is safe to say, however, that it will work only if both parents are stable and mature and enter into it with good will and the best interests of their child at heart. As Judge Breitel says, "Joint custody is for relatively stable, amicable parents behaving in a mature, civilized fashion."

Joint custody sounds as though it should suit the needs of certain modern families and, in theory, some parents and children in joint arrangements have the best of both worlds. The parents are still close to their children on a regular basis but not overwhelmed by laundry, dirty dishes, or brothers and sisters fighting. Children who are shared probably don't concern themselves with a secret fantasy that one of their parents didn't want them.

A Time for Soul Searching

At this very emotional time, parents are often unaware of some of their motivations. If they are thinking of joint custody, they must search their souls and try to be honest with themselves. Parents who choose joint custody either out of guilt over the divorce or inability to end their relationship might be making life worse for the children. "Let your guilt mobilize you to do what is best for your children," says child psychiatrist Dr. Richard Gardner. This means staying as actively involved as possible with the children but not taking joint custody where it may only bring more conflict, disruption, or disappointment to the family.

Four questions are crucial: 1. In your family (as in most, experts say), is one of you the "psychological parent," the parent whom the children are closer to and whom they would miss intensely if they were with their other parent for half of their time? 2. Will your children feel secure in a living arrangement of comings and goings, packing and unpacking, where those who must move back and forth—either parents or children—never feel entirely settled or stable? 3. Do you have the kind of relationship with your former spouse that will make the necessary frequent contact possible without excessive conflict? And, most of all, 4. Do you want and have time for the degree of work and responsibility of joint custody which includes the same cooking, cleaning, nurturing, disciplining, ministering duties of one-parent custody?

If after thinking through these questions, you believe that joint custody makes sense, it may be the arrangement for you and your family.

Chapter Seven

SPLIT CUSTODY

"Children form a unit within the family and can help each other out when parents break up. They are resources to one another," says Dr. Derdeyn.

What Is It?

In a split (or divided) custody arrangement, however, children cannot help one another out as they can in other arrangements because they are not kept together. Instead each parent takes full custody of at least one child of the marriage. Split custody is most typically used where one parent is either transferred by his company, is with the armed services, returns to his or her former hometown, or, for some other reason, will be living too far away from the rest of the family to make regular visits. Most parents and experts feel that separating children after a marital breakup causes them a double loss, first their parent, then their brother or sister, and that it generally should be avoided.

Situations Where Split Custody Might Work

A few experts say that there may be times when split custody would be appropriate. "Every family is different," says Dr. Levy. "Suppose the children are three and fourteen, they're not going to have the kind of relationship that kids have who are closer together."

"Alliances develop within a family," explains another psychiatrist, Dr. Robert Ravich, who suggests that special relationships can exist between a parent and a particular child. Ravich advises considering children's age, sex, whether they are the first, middle, or youngest, and their relationships with one another and with their parents when planning custody. Where there are three children, for example, Ravich suggests that if parents decide they want split custody, they should consider placing the middle child exclusively with one parent. The "middle child rule" is based on the theory that middle children can be and often feel neglected. While birth order affects some children a great deal, however, it is not necessarily more important than other factors such as age and sex.

"If there is an older boy around the age of ten or eleven," says another psychiatrist, "and a younger girl, the boy might go with the father, the girl with the mother."

A Forced Option

When comparing the two alternatives of split custody vs. one parent being so far away that he cannot see his child or children, Dr. Derdeyn commented, "We're talking about bad or worse here. Neither of these solutions is good."

The Wrong Reason for Choosing Split Custody

One day, some time after his separation, Howard said angrily to his wife, "I've already given you too much— more than you deserve. You're not getting all three children too."

As sometimes happens in families of divorce, Howard had lumped the children together with the other possessions and was treating the custody issue as part of the property settlement. When he moved to New York from California, he took his eldest child, David, and left ten-year-old Gail and seven-year-old Steven with his wife in Los Angeles. David was a normally temperamental twelve-year-old who had been having his problems getting along with his mother at the time. He welcomed the chance to get away. "My dad lets me do more. I think I'll like it better this way," he told me before he left.

Soon after Howard began his new, higher level job in New York which involved a fair amount of entertaining and travel as well as long working hours, he found that he didn't have the time for David which he had hoped to have. Nor did he have friends or family to turn to. When a problem came up in David's school, it was ten days before Howard could find the time to meet with the teacher as she had asked.

Six months after leaving California, Howard came home one night at ten-thirty to find David on the stoop of the brownstone adjacent to where they lived. He had not let the baby-sitter in when she arrived at her usual four o'clock starting time and had been out with his "friends" since five. He had had potato chips and soda for dinner, was smoking (with difficulty) a nonfilter cigarette, and hadn't done his homework.

David had been telling his father that he missed his mother, his sister and brother, his friends, his old school, and his swim team. After the incident on the late evening, Howard decided that it would be better to let the boy go back home.

Split/Joint Custody

A modified version of split custody, what we will call split/joint custody, occurs when siblings live with different parents for some of the time and live together (and with one of their parents) for a significant portion of the time as well.

When Carla and Bill Armstrong separated, both knew that they didn't want to give up custody entirely. Since Bill had just accepted a teaching position at a small college forty miles away, joint custody on an equal-time basis seemed impractical because of the children's schooling.

The parents talked about it with their three children, Louise, thirteen; Amelia, eleven; and Matthew, seven. The girls (who had always been close) were taking ballet, orchestra, and gymnastics in school, had many friends, and wanted to live at home with their mother, stay in the same school, and spend weekends and vacations with their father.

Matthew, a second-grader, had just started in a new elementary school after his neighborhood was redistricted, which meant he had been separated from most of the friends he had made in first grade. He said he didn't mind moving, that he wanted to live with his father, but would like to be with his mother and sisters on weekends.

The Armstrongs worked out a variation of split and joint custody that worked as follows: Louise and Amelia lived with their mother and Matthew with his father, during the week. Every Friday after work, Carla drove to her former husband's apartment, one week to drop off the girls who would spend the weekend with their father and Matthew, and, on alternate Fridays to pick up Matthew and have all the children with her for the weekend. Sunday evenings meant that Bill either returned Louise and Amelia or picked up Matthew.

Several months into this arrangement, Louise observed, "We do more things with our parents now than we used to. It seems as though they mean more to us and we mean more to them now."

Matthew said he liked living with his father and liked his new school but "sometimes I miss Amelia and Louise, especially Amelia. We used to play a lot of games and things." An occasional problem arises when Louise, who is beginning to go to parties and on group dates, doesn't want to go to her father's, but with the parents being fairly tolerant, the arrangement seems to be going smoothly.

Where divorced parents are to be separated by a great distance, they are working under difficult circumstances in deciding on a custody arrangement. They may have little choice in what they do. But children can be surprisingly strong and resilient, especially where they get the love and care they need from a parent.

Chapter Eight

WHAT'S BEST FOR YOU?

Custody decisions are complex, far-reaching, and usually influenced by conscious as well as unconscious motivations.

More and more fathers, in addition to most mothers, who divorce think about having custody. Because so many factors combine to make different custody arrangements more or less suitable for different families, it might be helpful to look at some of the specific circumstances and parental characteristics which make one-parent, joint, or split custody appropriate for some and not for others.

If You're Thinking About One-Parent Custody:

1. Do you believe that you are the "psychological parent" of your children? (Experts at the Yale

Child Study Center now say that in almost every family, there is clearly one parent who is the psychological parent.)

2. Are you and your spouse bitter toward one another or not on cooperative terms? (If so, joint custody would be unwise.)

3. Do you *like* having children around, not just your own, but their friends too? Do you mind feeding them and cleaning up after them?

4. Do you have the patience and the determination to discipline and train children so that they have a sense of order in their lives and so that they:

   (a) learn to do things for themselves (bathe, brush their teeth, take care of their clothes, do their homework, practice the piano, handle money);

   (b) learn acceptable, polite behavior and can handle themselves in social situations; and,

   (c) learn to be considerate of and helpful to you, to each other, and to others? These may sound like simple tasks but they will require years of perseverance on your part.

5. Can you remove splinters, treat wounds, pull loose teeth, give tepid baths when fevers run high, give shampoos?

6. More importantly, can you handle emotional wounds or problems? Do your children find you sensitive to their feelings and, therefore, trust you and confide in you? Essentially, do you connect with them emotionally?

7. Can you allow them a certain amount of childish behavior—crying, being jealous of a sister or brother, bad dreams, anxiety—without becoming angry?

8. Are you affectionate and physical with your children?

9. Can you cook—fix breakfasts during the morning rush, pack lunches, and prepare nutritious meals offering more variety than hamburgers and spaghetti?

10. Are you willing to handle housework—laundry, marketing, cleaning kitchens and bathrooms, vacuuming, picking up after the children, sewing torn seams, replacing buttons, ironing a shirt or dress for a special occasion—and give up the eight to ten hours a week necessary to take care of these things?

11. If you work full-time, can you be home for a reasonable amount of time during the week when the children are home? For example, can you be with them for dinner on at least three out of five weekday evenings?

12. Do you have, or know where to find, someone reliable, kind and intelligent to be there when the children come home from school, someone who can stay if you have to work late?

13. Can you take time off from work if one of your children is sick, has a day off, or is on vacation from school? If not, do you have a good substitute?

14. Can you attend a fair number of PTA meetings and parent-teacher conferences? Can you get away for some daytime school events, such as class plays, field days, and the like. Will you volunteer occasionally for some of the many jobs parents are called upon to do to help make the school run smoothly?

15. Can you drop everything and leave work if the

school calls and says your child has a temperature or just vomited in the classroom?

16. Are you willing to try and cope with a child saying to you, "If my parents hadn't gotten a divorce, maybe I would do better in school," ("maybe I would be happier") ("maybe I wouldn't be overweight") . . . ?

17. How do you feel about having your personal life secondary to your parental responsibilities: being able to meet fewer people socially; at times, having to cancel plans at the last minute because one of your children is sick or the baby-sitter can't make it; having a limited sex life?

18. Do you know that you will probably feel that you never have *enough* money, quiet, adult conversation, sex, *time*—time to be with your children, to concentrate on your work, to keep the house in order, to go out with friends?

19. Do you know that, in spite of all your work, you probably won't get much appreciation?

20. Do you feel that your children are special and irresistible? That having them with you will make all the sacrifices worthwhile?

21. Are you willing to take on whatever emotional problems your children may have in reaction to the separation, at a time when you, yourself, may not be feeling too strong?

22. Do you feel that you should assume exclusive custody because you are the more loving, more responsible, better parent?

23. Have you asked your children what living arrangement they would like? This is essential where children are approximately ten or older. Even younger children should be consulted,

106

although their opinions should not be controlling.

If You're Thinking About Joint Custody:

1. Do you sincerely believe that both of you have an equally close emotional bond with your children? That you share the role of "psychological parent" and are not depriving them of being with the one parent who really is the closer to the children—the one they talk to, trust, love, and depend on more than the other. (Parents often report having overheard their children ask each other, "Who do you like better, Mommy or Daddy?" with the children giving thoughtful but very definite answers.) Many others feel that one parent should almost always be given the dominant role, because joint custody, with its dual living arrangements, puts too great a strain on children. It is often too disruptive for young children and frequently doesn't last long with teen-agers who generally want to live in one place—where their friends and social lives are, where they can bring friends, and where they have a calm, stable life during what are difficult years.
2. Do neither of you want full-time custody?
3. Do both of you work outside the home?
4. Do you have a *good* working relationship with your former spouse?
5. Are you prepared to talk to him/her as often as every day to discuss your mutual responsibilities regarding the children—school, health care, dis-

cipline, extracurricular activities, dates with friends?

6. Do you live within a few miles of your former spouse?

7. Are you prepared for the inconvenience of your child moving in and out every few days, every week, or every month?

8. Can you handle all of the responsibilities mentioned under one-parent custody? While you will not have the children full-time, you will have them enough of the time so that you will have to provide full parental services—physical, emotional, intellectual, social. If your children are with you for roughly 50 percent of the time, that time with you is part of their real life and should not have the off-schedule tone that is often the case when children "visit" a noncustodial parent for a day or weekend.

9. Do you see joint custody as the best compromise you feel you can get? (This can be a valid reason for joint custody.)

10. What living arrangement do your children say they would like?

If You're Thinking About Split Custody:

1. How will your children feel about being separated from one another and how difficult will it be for them? Remember, children lend each other support and they can be especially helpful to each other following a separation.

2. Have you thought about how many other ad-

justments this will involve for your child at the same time he must cope with your divorce? Will he have to:
- (a) move to a new home? a new part of the country?
- (b) change schools?
- (c) give up most friends?
- (d) learn a new language?

3. Have you explored other, less drastic arrangements and found them unworkable (such as split/joint custody—see 9.)?

4. Have you thought about the recommendations on split custody of some psychiatrists who say that:
   - (a) If there are three children in your family, you might consider separating the middle, sometimes more neglected, child and leave the oldest and youngest together;
   - (b) where there is an older boy and a younger girl, the boy might go with the father and the girl with the mother?

5. Are your children more than six years apart in age? (This would probably make the separation easier on them.)

6. Are you and your former spouse going to be separated by a great distance? If the distance between you would prohibit anything more than one trip a year, this strengthens the argument for split custody—provided the children are not very close.

7. Do you realize that children can provide help and support to a custodial parent, thereby improving the home atmosphere for all? Older

children often help with and act as surrogate parents to younger children. Breaking up the children precludes this support system.

8. Do you in any way think of your children as possessions? Could it be that, without realizing it, you feel that having custody of none of the children would be "giving" too much to your spouse, and for that reason, you want split custody?

9. If you're contemplating a variation of split custody, what we call *split/joint custody*, do the following criteria apply:

    (a) Do you both want custody of one or more of the children with all the time, work, and responsibility that it entails?

    (b) Will you be living too far apart to allow a realistic joint-custody arrangement?

    (c) Are your children willing (and do you believe it wouldn't hurt them) to be split up?

    (d) Can you arrange for the children to be together on weekends or some other regular basis?

Each of the custody arrangements discussed here has worked successfully for some children and parents. The point to custody is to choose the arrangement that will work best for you and your children and which, in turn, will probably bring out the best in you as a parent— whether you are the single or joint custodian or the visiting parent.

You may want to talk over some of the points on the custody checklist with your wife or husband, spelling out the three to four hours a week necessary for washing, drying, folding and putting away laundry, the homework to supervise each evening, the one evening or the Saturday morning which must be given over to supermarket shopping and other errands for the week, the baths, the lessons, the haircuts, and so on that go with having custody. Where you are somewhat unsure about custody but not hostile toward one another, this discussion can help to clarify your thinking. If you are already in general agreement, it will help to reassure you both.

On the other hand, where you disagree radically, any checklist discussion might only provide new points to argue about. If this happens, you might suggest talking things over with a third party—a family counselor, psychiatrist, psychologist, or a clergyman experienced in these matters—someone who will help you reach a realistic plan.

With the backup of an objective professional, talking about some of the specific points on the checklist might help defuse some of the emotion surrounding divorce and custody: Do you *like* having children around? Do your children trust and confide in you? Can you cook, clean, sew, and iron or are you willing to learn? Do you have some flexibility in your work schedule to allow for the children sometimes needing you after school or during the day? Will you subordinate your social and sex life to your parental responsibilities? Where will you both live? What kind of working relationship will you have together? How many new adjustments are you asking your child to make as part of the custody arrangement in addition to adjusting to the separation? Do you think of your children as possessions?

If you arrive at the most suitable arrangement, you might be surprised at what a good single or joint custodian or part-time noncustodial parent you will be.

Chapter Nine

CUSTODY AND THE STAGES OF DIVORCE

Gloria arrived late at her gynecologist's office for a ten o'clock appointment, her eyes swollen and her face drawn. Dr. Fisher asked her if anything was the matter.

"My husband told me last night that he wants a divorce," Gloria explained. "He said he felt trapped, that he was stagnating. He wants to take a sabbatical from teaching and go out West to work on his writing. I . . . I knew things weren't great, but I never expected this," she added in tears. "I'm thirty-seven years old and I feel like my life is over.

"Then there are the children. I don't know how I'm going to handle them. . . . Oh, hell. What a mess."

"In my practice," Dr. Fisher said, "I've seen so many women in your position and it happened to me too. Going through a divorce has to be one of the toughest experiences there is."

The Stress Factor

Indeed, psychologists say that ending a marriage and starting a new life is a more stressful experience than having surgery, getting married, having a baby, starting a new job, or going through any other life crisis except the death of a child or a spouse. To make matters worse, the separating man or woman and their children usually feel very much alone. Society gives lip service to its acceptance of divorce, yet leaves the families of divorce alone to cope with their anxieties, loneliness, and financial problems. In fact, society provides far more services to a person out of a job than to someone out of a marriage, even though the latter may have greater financial and psychological problems.

Public agencies, schools, even family doctors have not sufficiently addressed this problem which threatens the mental health of so many.

While divorce is often an intelligent step which can lead to a more productive, happy life and may preserve the mental health of children by removing them from a hateful environment, the divorce process will for a time awaken some of the deepest fears and conflicts which we all experience and which each of us has only partially resolved—guilt, shame, mistrust, fear of abandonment. So, it is in a self-doubting, vulnerable position that parents and children face the many stresses of separation and divorce and the responsibilities of custody.

For you as a parent, those stresses not only include losing a relationship and a way of life in which you invested so much of yourself, but several accompanying crises as well, each carrying its own high stress factor: having less money; possibly having to move to a smaller home and a new community; finding a job, or, managing a job you already have along with more responsibilities at home; losing some of your old friends; feeling frustrated sexually; and hardest of all, dealing with your children's adjustment. They will miss their other parent, have to spend more time alone, possibly have to make financial sacrifices and deal with their own guilt, anger, depression, and other problems. They will need you more than ever, but you may be at your weakest.

Psychologists call separation a trauma. Just as an automobile accident or an operation cause physical trauma to the body, the stress of separation and divorce impair your *emotional* functioning—your sleep, your concentration, your ability to work, your memory, your sense of optimism, and your relationships with others. Especially your children.

As an injured body heals gradually, the psyche too recovers from a shock slowly. While in the early part of the process, it may seem that the pain (some people have called it plain terror) will never stop, you will eventually regain your emotional equilibrium. We can call the steps back to full emotional strength the "stages" of divorce.

Unfortunately, few of the many parents who go through separation and divorce are prepared for the emotional difficulties they will face. Yet, how they handle them will have a critical effect on their own and their children's adjustment.

After Separation, What Lies Ahead?

Because so many thousands of parents and children join the separated and divorced ranks each week, it is a shame that more of them don't know what to expect—

and what to look forward to. I have looked into answers to some questions which parents have told me would have been of help to them had they known them in the early stages of their separation. While they say these answers couldn't have prevented most of their pain, they feel that certain information would have comforted them and their children and would have given them hope.

Emotional Divorce

As a general rule, your divorce adjustment will be easier when you want to end the marriage and hardest when you *don't* want to. Other factors such as your age, your children's ages, your job skills, how much money you have, your interests, how long you were married, and whether you have good friends will affect your adjustment. Women who have been studied generally report that they suffer more stress before the actual decision to separate while men report greater stress symptoms—sleep disturbances, loneliness, drinking, and work problems—during the period immediately following separation.

On the average, researchers say, men tend to adjust to separation and divorce more quickly than women in the sense that they can usually meet new people, become involved in new interests, and generally reorganize their lives to adapt to the separation quicker, while women, particularly housewives, not having the structure and contacts which come with a job, and usually having more home and child-related responsibilities, must virtually invent a new life for themselves—often one which they have had no experience with. They must make radical changes in their day to day existence if they are to become integrated into the economic, legal and social parts of society and build new lives.

Yet, in spite of men's advantages some experts point out special emotional problems which they may have in dealing with divorce. Dr. David Chiraboga points out that the way in which boys are often raised ("Big boys don't cry") can lead to "a wall between men and their emotions," while early social experience "allows women comparatively free access." He goes on to say that "the shock of experiencing fully their own emotional state may have a devastating effect on the men," with a "frequent use of such buffers as work or excessive social activity" in order to avoid the problems and the feelings which come with divorce. "Women," Chiraboga feels, "more in touch with their emotional life . . . may hit an emotional low more quickly, but may also be faster in resolution."[1]

To some degree, virtually everyone will go through the stages of divorce which most separated and divorced people describe, and which usually take from two to four years to recover from.

The first stage in the sometimes rocky journey from being a "happily" married parent to being a contentedly single parent may begin while you are still married. It often includes recurring depressed or angry feelings and an awareness that the marriage is failing, alternating with hopes that things will get better . . . when the kids are all in school . . . when we have more money . . . if I get a job.

In this first stage, called by some psychologists "emotional divorce," you and your spouse will probably begin to talk less, touch less, and, in general, hold back more and more feeling, until, at some point, you break up.

"When we finally separated, my wife and I had become strangers in certain ways" is the way one man described it. "We were aloof. The intimacy was gone."

The Next Stage: Rebuilding Your Life

The stage of "emotional divorce" is probably the most difficult one, *especially* around the time of the physical separation when the children are feeling at their worst too. But once you've gotten through the depressed, slowed-down feeling of this period, you may not be in the clear yet.

While you may no longer have any love for your spouse, you may still feel enough anger to want to fight with him and punish him. Money battles and custody and visitation disputes often come up here. If you settle into a cozy nest with your anger and spend your time getting back at your spouse, you can't build the new life you need. Eventually, your attachment to your former spouse should diminish to the point that you no longer are preoccupied with hurt or anger over it.

Once you have your own household, you will probably find that you're learning to be a more effective single parent and are delegating more responsibility to your children than you ever thought possible before. Your priorities probably will have changed to the point that having a spotless kitchen is less important than spending prime evening time with your children.

You may have a new job by now. A few words of hard-learned experience from other single parents might interest you. A job which offers some financial independence, a feeling of accomplishment, and an opportunity to be in a stimulating environment can be highly therapeutic, especially for someone newly separated. But be cautious. Don't overwork yourself to the point of fatigue and resentment.

Single parents who have lived through the strains of making a living and making a home stress the relationship between physical strength and emotional well-being. While this may seem self-evident, many single parents feel it should be emphasized that, especially at this time, when you have added responsibilities as well as emotional strains, you should be religious about: eating *healthful* foods (avoid sweets and starches as much as possible), getting *enough sleep*, and *exercising*. (Psychologists have said that jogging and other exercise routines can counteract depressed feelings.)

Some recently separated parents with custody of their children have found that highly demanding full-time jobs can be too much to handle while children are young.

"I would become exhausted, then I would get angry at having to do so much. Before long, I found myself on the phone in a heated battle with my former husband, accusing him of being stingy and threatening to go to court. My children would get upset because we were arguing when what they needed was peace and relief from the fighting," explained one mother.

One father said, "Sometimes, I found myself so tired that I wouldn't do anything except go to work, take care of the house and kids, and watch television." (Experts have called television an addiction that probably should be taken as moderately as alcohol, drugs, and sweets.) If you're finding work and home responsibilities to be too much but don't want to give up your job, consider taking in a boarder in exchange for something toward the rent or the mortgage and some help with housework and baby-sitting or sharing a larger home with someone in your situation in order to cut expenses and spread the work-load. And delegate whatever chores you can to the children.

The other cautionary note concerning work is more subtle. Working full-time and raising children can be a kind of escape from loneliness, but at the same time can stand in the way of your getting out and developing a social life. With your hours and energy consumed by a job, children and a house, you won't have time to do anything else. But it is important that your life not be all work and sacrifice. Your children should see you going out with friends of both sexes, attending parties, or going to clubs or courses. (See the chapter in Part Six on Dating.) They will feel bad for you if you seem lonely and cloistered and may even come to feel guilty about going out with their friends or enjoying themselves with their other parent.

"After a while, I found I was getting more of what I wanted to do accomplished," explained a working mother who was recently divorced. "I cut out the time-wasters, the luxuries that I used to enjoy but that really weren't doing much for me—having long conversations on the telephone (now I rarely talk more than five minutes), watching television (if I watch for a half an hour before I go to sleep, that's a lot). When you cut out those two things," she went on, "you have several more hours in the day. Now, I find I can do my job, spend time with the children and go out one, sometimes two evenings a week. I also try to get extra sleep on weekends. Sure, once in a while I'm tired," she admitted, "but not usually and I find that I thrive on the activity and stimulation my life gives me. It's what works best for me."

As this woman did, many parents with exclusive or joint custody find that organizing the many parts of their lives is difficult in the beginning, but that most problems can be ironed out and new routines established to fit their schedules. And most parents seem to feel that a job helps a great deal in getting them through the emotional, economic, and legal strains of divorce.

Chapter Ten

THE NEW CUSTODY ARRANGEMENT: HOW WILL THE CHILDREN REACT?

(Jeff, 9): "Some of the kids whose parents got divorced are sad. They don't want to go to school, they don't care about anything. Some are so mad they're going crazy. And some kids try real hard to pretend it doesn't bother them."

No matter what custody arrangement you settle on, with whatever special effects that arrangement may have on your children, there are certain psychological reactions that are common to *all* children of divorce. Parents should be prepared to help their children cope with them.

Few children of the nearly million and a half divorced couples each year had enjoyed ideal, loving, tranquil home lives before the breakup. Yet, contradictory as it may seem, these children tend to be especially vulnerable to the shock and separation of divorce. One reason is that because of the turmoil and insecurities with which many of them lived, they were not able to build the strength they need to cope with crisis. Add to that parents who may not have resolved their anger, hurt, or bitterness over the divorce. In the real world of divorce it's hard to stop the fighting. Revenge can be satisfying and depression is common. It becomes easy to see why children have a difficult time adjusting to their new lives and custody arrangements.

At few times in a parent's life will he or she feel the range of emotions, the uncertainty about the future, or the financial concerns that come with a marital separation. At the same time, parents are told to control their anger and anxieties, get their lives together and keep the children's lives as healthy, happy, and normal as possible. Surprisingly this responsibility can be therapeutic. "If I didn't have the kids depending on me I would have hit rock bottom" said one mother. "The best thing for me during the year after my separation was that I had to keep busy taking care of them."

Parents who have lived through the experience of separation and divorce and many professionals who have helped them will readily agree that the reactions of children to divorce, which will be discussed on the following pages—regression, grief, guilt, denial, psychosomatic and nervous symptoms, lack of self-esteem—are common to children experiencing a major life crisis, and that in a divorce these reactions tend to be *most* acute: (1) at the time of the physical separation when one parent is moving out; (2) for as long as *open conflict* between parents continues; and, (3) where one parent loses touch with or loses interest in the children.

Following a separation parents should expect some temporary emotional setbacks in their children's be-

124

havior, as children struggle to cope with the stress. Parents should be on the alert for more serious problems as well and keep in mind that their child's development is a continuing *process* and that certain reactions to the split might not occur immediately but may appear at a future time.

Children will respond to a disruption in their family according to their age and developmental level as well as to the strengths, weaknesses, and idiosyncrasies of their individual personalities.

Before discussing them in detail we will look first at the major symptoms of separation and divorce as they affect children of different age groups.

The Infant-Toddler

The child who is not yet talking fluently is still affected by what is going on in his home. Where there is marital discord, tension usually affects parents and the way they relate to their baby. If they are angry or overwrought it will show in how they behave. A baby in such circumstances will not be as relaxed as he might be.

The Preschool Child

Children between the ages of two and five fall into two general behavior groups. The younger group approximately between two and three and a half years will usually react to family breakdown by regressing to more babyish behavior—increased crying, whining, separation problems, aggressiveness, and overall crankiness. The three-and-a-half- to five-year-olds may also become crankier, regress in their toilet training and, as they begin to sense the consequences of things, they will often ask for their absent parent while being afraid that the parent they are living with might leave too. They will probably blame themselves—something they did or said, the fact that they wouldn't eat or that they hit their sisters or brothers, or whatever—for the separation.

The School-Age Child

These children too may show more immature behavior for a while—whining, crying, fighting. Unlike younger children they will understand better the reasons for the divorce and be less likely to blame themselves although there will probably be some guilt. These children seem better able to organize their own lives in a way that helps them deal with their loss—they have school, friends, and interests to protect them. They tend to be less likely than younger (and sometimes older) children to have their development seriously impaired.

The Adolescent

The trials and pressures of the teen-age years—to break away from home and parents, to handle their emerging sexuality, and to establish themselves as heterosexuals, to make plans for the future—are difficult enough for a youngster with a calm, stable home life. When the home is disrupted the teen-ager is under even more pressure. Getting caught in the middle of a divorce will often prevent the teen-ager from getting on with the important tasks of his own development and can have serious long-

126

term consequences. If he is to survive, he must remove himself from his home atmosphere more abruptly than he would have liked to.[1]

Very broadly speaking these are the general reactions of children to separation and divorce. There is a great deal parents can do, however, to exacerbate or to alleviate some of these symptoms, a discussion of which will follow. But first, it is important to look deeper into some of the behavioral problems and the reasons behind them which some children of divorce have.

Guilt

When her parents told her they were separating, Michelle, four, said that she knew her father was leaving "because I act dumb." One year later when her teacher was going over some phonics work in kindergarten class and called on Michelle to answer a question, the child repeated the same guilty belief. "I'm too dumb to learn that. My daddy left because I'm dumb." Michelle's mother, at a loss to understand her daughter's feelings, learned more about them from a child psychologist.

"A child often sees divorce as his punishment for having been bad," he explained. "Bad" to a child can mean: hitting his sister too often, playing ball in the house, spilling his milk, not liking his piano lessons, not reading well enough, or asserting himself too much at the price of his parents' love. This reaction is most common to children roughly between the ages of three and seven who are less able to understand divorce or to separate their own lives from their parents', although guilty reactions can still be found in older children.

The logical conclusion of thinking "the divorce is my

fault" is "I can undo it." In efforts to reunite their parents, children often will promise to be good all the time, threaten to run away from home, or never come out of their room, and the like.

"Some guilt in reaction to crisis," says Dr. Derdeyn "is almost universal among all of us. We never get over that." When something goes wrong it is common that we blame ourselves to some degree, thinking "if only I had . . ." Most young children's feelings of guilt over their parents' divorce do not indicate deep-rooted problems and should have greatly diminished after a period of months.

Guilt in fact may help cushion the blow for children in the early period. First, it offers them a rational explanation for something which otherwise seems frighteningly arbitrary to a child who can't understand the subtleties of relationships. ("It's my fault. If it's not my fault then why did it happen? Maybe other terrible things will happen.")

Reassuring children again and again the divorce is not their fault and therefore that they can't "fix" it should help them gradually to accept the fact that their parents' marriage is really over. If they are unwilling or unable to, which is most likely in families where intense conflict has continued after the separation and had been the case for a long time preceding it, consult a child therapist.

Fantasizing

Parents should keep in mind that virtually no child of divorce ever entirely gives up his secret hope for his parents' reconciliation. Even if that hope lives only in his fantasies.

When his parents finally divorced after months of a

bitter separation and court battle, Jason, five, wouldn't acknowledge the truth. Instead, he told his teacher and his classmates that his father was coming back home soon to live with him and that "Mommy and Daddy won't be divorced anymore."

Because of this tendency be careful what you say when you are around your children and try to present consistent information. If you give them confusing signals they can easily be misled and disappointed.

After a November Sunday spent with his father, five-year-old Jeffrey came home and asked his mother, "Mommy, what are we going to do for Christmas?"

His mother answered, "Honey, you know Grandma and Grandpa are staying with us and Uncle Bill and Aunt Helen will come by with the children."

"But Daddy says we should all be together so why can't we? I want Daddy to come."

"Well, your Daddy and I are separated, Jeff, so we can't. And your father knows that and shouldn't have told you differently. You'll see him at his house on Christmas Eve."

There are children who find it difficult or impossible to express their feelings about their parents' separation directly but may give important clues to what they are thinking through their fantasy play. Some, who feel frustrated and powerless because of their parents breaking up, may use toys, dolls, blocks, or drawings depicting helpless animals or people being attacked by monsters or overwhelmed by storms. Through fantasy games such as "house" or "dolls" children often express secret wishes like "Mommy and Daddy are in bed together" or "Mommy and Daddy are taking their children ice skating."

Such fantasies offer parents insight into children's

thinking and the opportunity to reassure and comfort them. Saying something like "I know you wish this was how our family was right now" gives a child an opening to talk about how he feels, about his worries, fears, anger, and lets him know that you understand and sympathize. You can also remind a child in a gentle way that while his thought is a happy one, "When everyone in our family lived in the same house we weren't very happy and there was a lot of fighting." This may help him realize that his fantasies are far from the reality and may also help him to talk more openly.

Psychosomatic and Nervous Symptoms

Todd, eleven, had never performed well during school exams and was nervous each year before starting a new class. But after his parents' separation he became worse. He developed colitis and often was too ill with severe cramps to go to school on days when he had to take a test or give an oral report.

Martha refused to visit her father, saying that each time after she came home she developed terrible headaches which lasted for hours. Jack reported that his asthma got much worse following his visits with his father, but added quickly, "I don't get asthma attacks because of my father."

Some children, most often those between the ages of ten and thirteen, react to the stress of divorce with physical problems such as stomachaches and headaches. In other children, separation can trigger nervous symptoms such as stuttering, tics, nightmares, not being able to sleep, or phobias like a fear of heights or of not wanting to go out alone.

130

Eating and especially overeating is another symptom. It often indicates a craving for love or security or excessive anxiety. Wallerstein and Kelly talk about Kate, who had begun overeating after her parents separated and were locked in a custody battle. At one point Kate warned her therapist, "You better not ask me about the divorce . . . I'll get hungry."

Each of these symptoms is a clear sign of trouble and a cry for help that should be responded to, probably with the kind of professional help discussed in Part Five, if it persists more than a few months.

Lack of Self-Esteem

"I was divorced when my son was three. He's now twenty-one," a woman told me. "He was fine during the early years. I explained the reasons for the divorce to him and he accepted them. He did well in school. But then his father moved away, remarried, and they almost never saw each other.

"The problems came later, when he was a teen-ager. He had trouble making friends with both boys and girls. When I would suggest that he go out he would say, 'Why should I bother? They won't like me anyway.' He *expected* to be rejected.

"Brad felt his father had rejected him (and the truth is his father *did* reject him). Oh, he would call him every once in a while and ask how school was, but that was never Brad's problem. He was always a good student. (He needed his father to care about him, which his father really didn't do. Consequently he felt bad about himself— that he wasn't likable.)

"Finally when Brad went away to college he went into a

deep depression. His marks weren't nearly what they should have been. When we talked on the phone he told me that he spent most of his time in his room. When he came home at Christmas I said, 'All right. You need a man to talk to. You can't talk to me that much about it. Let's get some professional help.'

"He had a good person here at home. When he went back to school he didn't like the first psychologist he found but was happy with the second. He's now much more content and seems to have worked out a lot of his problems.

"After a while Brad and I could talk more openly too. One day we were talking about why his father didn't pay enough attention to him. I didn't try to hide anything. I said, 'Your father is not a friendly person. He doesn't have friends himself.' "

Divorce can lower a child's self-esteem in many subtle ways. Where a child is preoccupied with his parents' continued warring or with a depressed parent at home, he won't be able to concentrate fully in school and may fall down in his work, he may be troubled or irritable or lose touch with his friends or get in with the wrong group. Soon, without realizing it, he may become a poor student, a discipline problem or anti-social, and eventually believe he can do no better.

Sadness, Depression

"Daddy, why didn't you want me to live with you?" asked eight-year-old Phillip during a Saturday morning breakfast at his father's apartment.

"I *would* like you to be living with me all the time, Phil," answered the boy's father. "But your mother and I decided that you and Jenny would be better off in the house with her. I work all day and I couldn't spend much time with you during the week. But you know I do love you."

Even where children are reasonably satisfied with the custody arrangement their parents decide on, most can't help occasionally feeling that their noncustodial parent may not have wanted them.

Like Phil, they may need the kind of reassurance his father gave him along with plenty of time and love to realize that this is not so.

Then there are those children who suffer a more pervasive sadness. Six-year-old Jimmy said he didn't cry about his parents' divorce "because if I start, I won't be able to stop."

One-third of the children of divorce are depressed. They tend to exhibit accident-prone behavior, are unconcerned about their safety, or have suicidal fantasies. It is important to understand that children often show depression differently from grownups. They do not necessarily break into tears or behave in the quiet, withdrawn manner parents might expect. Overactivity and boisterousness can be symptoms of depression in a child as well as crying or sad withdrawal. When a child is obviously sad, withdrawn and depressed, or where he is unusually active and unable to relax, concentrate or channel his energies constructively, that is a signal for parents to get professional help for the child.

Anger

When parents separate, it makes children angry at the parent who has left them and anxious that their other parent will leave too. Many children of divorce are angry at their parents—usually because their parents made them sad, their parents weren't able to work out their problems, the divorce meant less money to go around, they no longer can go to camp or perhaps have the two-wheel bike they had been looking forward to—or because their life is no happier after the separation than it had been before.

An eight-year-old boy whose parents continued their fighting even though they separated said, "They said it was going to be better but it *isn't*. It's *worse!* They fight every day. It makes me *mad!*"

Children of divorce also get angry when their parents don't keep their promises. "It's bad enough they got divorced," one nine-year-old boy said to me. "But sometimes my father calls to cancel something we had planned at the last minute. Other times he calls when I have plans to do something else and he wants to see me *that* day. Even if I want to do the other thing with one of my friends or something, I go with my father. I know that if I say 'No' I might not get to see him for a long time. It's not fair though. He should give me some notice."

Most children have good reason to be angry when their parents break up. It is a punishment they didn't deserve and they have nothing to say in this decision which so deeply affects every aspect of their lives. It is important at this time to listen to their feelings and to be sympathetic and understanding of their anger. But children too must gradually learn to be sympathetic of others. Explain to them that the marriage, with the fighting, drinking, general unhappiness or whatever else it included, made *you* very sad. While they may not have wanted you to separate, they must remember that the adults in the family have feelings too.

Listening to and sympathizing with their feelings is

important. But once a separation has begun, trying to convince them that "We'll all feel better soon" and "We'll manage" are important next steps. As is making certain that you are still in charge. Don't let children's complaints about such things as having less money divert you from taking control of the situation and behaving rationally and not out of guilt. If the children can't go to summer camp or can't get the $250-set of drums at this time, let them know that you're sorry but that in order to be fair to everyone in the family you can't afford that now. Maybe at some point you will be able to. But in the meantime let's enjoy other things. You might encourage the children if they're old enough to get part-time work or think about a job for yourself. Be fair, cope and think optimistically.

Beware the "Model" Child

As a new separated parent you will have many pressures and worries to face in reorganizing your life. It is important to remember, though, that if your child acutely senses your many other concerns—related to finances, work, dating—he may try too hard not to be an additional burden sometimes at his own expense.

"Eric couldn't be better," his mother who had recently begun a new career as a real-estate saleswoman told me about her seven-year-old after the separation. "He insists that he can walk the five blocks to school alone so that I don't have to drive him and be late for work. It's great for me." Then she added, "If I'm rushed in the morning he turns on the stove and makes himself bacon and waffles. He's terrific. He's so independent. Just what I want," she said within Eric's earshot. "An independent kid."

One evening some time later Eric came into his mother's room crying. "What's the matter Eric?" his mother asked.

"There's this kid . . . I didn't tell you because I know you'll be mad . . . there's this kid who's been following me to school every day asking me for quarters . . . I've taken all the quarters from my bank but today he said that if I don't have seventy-five cents tomorrow he's going to smash my teeth in," Eric sobbed. "I don't have any more quarters and I don't want to walk to school myself, Mom."

"Oh my God, Eric, why didn't you tell me?" his mother asked, not realizing that in praising him for being independent beyond his years and ability, she might have been conveying the hidden message that he shouldn't burden her with a seven-year-old's problems.

It's easy enough to spot this problem where it exists. No child should be a model child. If your child is behaving too perfectly after your separation, maybe he's afraid that if he causes too much trouble you might leave too. These children need to know, *above all,* that the parent whom they live with cares about them, even if this means that the parent has to give up some outside interests or activities. "Parents," says Dr. Cobb, "must be willing to make a few sacrifices."

Rebelliousness

Questioning parental values is a normal part of adolescents' search for identity but when coupled with separation and divorce, this stage may temporarily include extreme defiance and a rejection of all parental values including those of education and work.

The New Custody Arrangement

"Parents may see a sudden reversal of roles," Sirgay Sanger says of teen-agers of divorce, "where the children become the critics and authority figures."

Fraser, a newly divorced and guilt-ridden father of four teen-agers, recognizes in John Updike's story "Domestic Life in America" that he "had forfeited his right to moral indignation and the boy knew it. The unspoken ground note of all his conversations with his children was Fraser's request for forgiveness."

Another danger for teen-agers of divorce is where they lose the stable, mature model of heterosexual relationships which they need.

Fourteen-year-old Vicki had been a good student and an outgoing, popular girl among her high-school sophomore classmates. But after her parents separated and her mother began an almost teen-age dating schedule, Vicki changed too. Her marks fell, she quit the school paper and the cheerleading squad and began keeping late hours with new friends who were known in school as fast kids. A friend commented that Vicki "is trying to keep up with her mother." It wasn't long before Vicki was drinking, smoking pot, and having sex with two different boys. One day an old girlfriend of hers pulled her aside in the school corridor. "I don't know if I should tell you this, Vicki, but Bruce just told me something he saw written on the mirror in the boys' room about you."

"What was it, tell me," Vicki said.

"Well . . . don't be mad. It said if you screwed Vicki like I screwed Vicki oh, oh, oh what a gal . . . and then it went on. It got more graphic."

Vicki ran out of the school and went straight home. She packed a suitcase, left a note for her mother who was working that she was going by train to her father's and would stay there through the Easter vacation, which was only a few days off.

137

Eventually Vicki's parents unravelled the story and recognized their own part in her problems. (Vicki's father led a hectic social life and hadn't wanted custody.) Both parents talked to a psychiatrist who recommended a professional for Vicki to see as well. Within a few weeks Vicki had returned to her mother's house and to school. She and her mother are both seeing therapists for what will probably amount to only a few months of treatment. And Vicki's outlook and behavior have improved greatly.

Divorce Can Have Positive Effects on Children

While children will have some bad reactions to parental divorce, the picture is not all bleak and frightening. In the long run the separation may result in more positive than negative effects.

When the Fighting Stops

Most parents are so busy worrying about what a "broken home" will do to their children that they don't realize the *relief* which the separation may provide. A child's emotional well-being depends less on whether he has an intact family than on the amount of conflict and tension he lives with at home. Children do better in a peaceful home with one parent than in an unhappy home with two parents and so does the parent.

The best thing parents can do for their child is to "put the war to rest," as one psychiatrist phrased it.

If parents keep one key point in mind it will ease their own guilt and stress and anger, and this in turn will help their children. According to the latest research and

138

experience of the professionals, the main factor in a child's adjustment to divorce is the *parents' ability to cooperate.*

Also vital for parents to remember are: not to denigrate their child's other parent in front of the child and to take the attitude that life has its adversities but that they can cope with them.

School and Your Child

Any adjustment problems which a child is having at home will probably carry over to school and affect his work, his behavior, or his friendships.

Where parents and school personnel keep each other informed, jointly following a child's progress, they can prevent or catch in its early stages any negative reaction to divorce which he may be having. This can be an invaluable aid to a family that is breaking up. For a time school may be the child's mainstay. He will need his teachers, his friends, and the structure which school provides more than he ever has before.

Teachers who are willing to exchange phone numbers or write letters to a child during vacations can be extremely helpful. You might ask the school to consider placing your child with a male teacher if his father is the parent whom he sees less.

Some teen-agers may go through a period of exaggerated rebelliousness which can carry over into their school work. This situation should not be allowed to persist without the guidance counselor or psychologist as well as the principal being called in immediately.

Teachers may see other problems in children whose parents were recently separated or divorced. Problems from severe depression to overaggressiveness and others. Again, the school in its front-line position can spot and try to deal with them before they become entrenched. But it is important that parents stay in close touch with the school.

Chapter Eleven

PART-TIME PARENTS

The main tragedy for a child of divorce is the fact that he will no longer see one of his parents as much as he needs to or would like to.

Children whose parents are separated depend almost entirely on the parent with whom they live for day-in, day-out love, guidance, and stability, but their other parent plays a crucial role in their lives. Or should. He or she can make a significant difference in the child's emotional health and growth. For the good or for the bad. (See section which follows: *Part-Time Parents Are Crucial.*) It is alarming that only one-third of the children from divorced homes see their fathers regularly.[1] Yet, it is somewhat understandable. Being a part-time parent can be frustrating, confusing, and challenging.

"The kids are tired of the zoo, they've been to the circus, they saw the latest movie three times already, it's too cold to play in the park and, with the alimony and child support I pay, I've only got twenty dollars to get me through the next three days, so I can't even take them out to dinner. On top of that, when I got to the house Saturday morning, John had a friend over, and when he saw me he said, 'Oh, it's *you* again, Dad.' I'm beginning to wonder whether it's worth it."

Not everyone believes it's worth the trouble for parents who have moved out of the house to stay involved with their children. "It creates friction when I see my ex-wife and we usually have a fight," says one father. "Now she leaves me waiting outside the door for the kids." Others have said, "The fathers would be better off starting a new family." But these people aren't fully understanding children's needs and rights.

Children are vulnerable and easily feel rejected, not good enough, or abandoned. "It's hard enough just being a child," explains one psychiatrist. "Most everyone is taller, stronger, faster at doing things, knows more, and is less clumsy than you are and it's easy to feel inadequate. Add to that parents fighting and breaking up, and many kids think that since Daddy left (the same would be true for Mommy), "Daddy doesn't like *me*." That can be a crushing blow to a child's fragile ego if something isn't done about it.

Part-Time Parents Are Crucial

Research demonstrates that fathers, as well as mothers, make an important contribution to children's healthy emotional development. Fathers tend to be more demanding of their children, more ambitious for them, and more concerned with how they adjust to their sex roles.

(Because one-parent families in the past have been primarily without fathers, most research has been done on so-called "father absence.") Many studies have shown the high rates of crime, drug use, school failure, promiscuity, and general underachievement among children with poor or nonexistent relationships with their fathers. Nor is it any surprise that children who do have close relationships with two parents form easier, more successful relationships with the opposite sex when they get older.

While lack of success is more common among people who have not had satisfying relationships with their fathers, many highly successful men and women, on the other hand, have attributed part of their success to strong, close relationships with their fathers.

Don't Become an Ex-Parent

Cutting a child off from a parent for any reason (except when there is a clear danger of the parent beating, seducing, neglecting, or severely harming him in some other way) can be so harmful to children's emotional health that it is worthwhile to go over some additional reasons why it is so important that ex-husbands or ex-wives not become ex-parents.

1. In the event of the death or serious illness of a custodial parent, a child would normally go to his other parent. The child's loss would be doubly traumatic if he had not had an ongoing relationship with that other parent. Imagine yourself as a child moving in with a stranger, or, worse, if you had heard nothing but negative ("Your father's a bum") or frightening ("He's a maniac") statements about him.

143

2. Not allowing a child to see his parent is, in the opinion of many lawyers and psychiatrists, a violation of the child's civil rights.

3. A child will fantasize exaggerated things about his parent into either an image of menace or glory. Some children spend inordinate amounts of their valuable time and energy thinking about their mysterious parents and some even go in search of them. And sooner or later a child will come to see his parents accurately. Letting him know about and see his parent—regardless of the parent's problems with alcohol, irresponsibility, thoughtlessness, or other flaws—and helping him come to grips with reality is what experts say is the healthiest method of dealing with it. Above all, it should prevent fantasies which can be more disturbing and emotionally disruptive than the truth.

4. Not seeing a parent can keep alive some of the guilt and poor self-esteem that probably came with the separation: "Daddy (or Mommy) doesn't want to see me, therefore, I'm not worth seeing" or "The divorce is my fault."

5. Not being close to a parent of the *same* sex deprives a child of an important role model in learning to be male or female. Not being close to a parent of the *opposite* sex deprives a child of the chance to learn to relate and understand that sex. Both relationships are important in later friendships and heterosexual attachments.

6. Preventing a child from seeing his parent can make the idea seem desirable, may encourage sneak visits, and will probably make the child more hostile to his custodial parent.

7. If a parent is not being allowed to see his child, he is more likely to challenge custody and initiate long, unpleasant legal battles, which are upsetting to a child.

8. When a child becomes a more aggressive, more sexually aware and temperamental preteen- and teenager, living with only one parent can make the period unnecessarily tense. Having a second parent around to talk to and spend time with can act as a safety valve to relieve some of the pressure.

9. When parents separate, this divides a child's loyalty. In order for the child not to feel "torn" or to develop a disturbing internal conflict, he should have as much chance as possible to see both parents.

10. Finally, having a mutually caring relationship with two parents will help a child bounce back from the shock and depression that may have come with the separation. That relationship will help both parents to recover as well (especially the parent who is living alone). Happier parents, in turn, will do more for their child.

Professor Watson writes, ". . . children need both parents . . . either parent's effort to thwart this need or in any way make it difficult or impossible, should be taken as evidence of parental apathy."

Problems of Being a Part-Time Parent

All right, you say. Fathers are important. Mothers are important. Perhaps especially so after the shock of a separation and divorce. But it can be almost impossible to maintain a close relationship with a child if the courts and your ex-spouse work against you. One frustrated father explained, "I don't get to see my son much. I have no say in who his friends are or where he goes to school. I didn't even know until the last minute that he was having his tonsils out!"

145

In spite of wide publicity given to those fathers who get custody of their children, the actual incidence of this happening is still very low. This is due, in part, to the fact that fathers are still believed by many to be the parent of secondary importance. This same thinking, often held by judges and former wives, can carry over to the way visitation is treated.

For years fathers have complained that while they are forced to make their support payments under threat of fines and jail, they have no guarantee that, in turn, their visitation rights will be honored or enforced.

In many states across the country, fathers' rights groups are slowly working to change that. Their efforts, combined with women's push toward equality on all fronts, are bringing about some change in the status quo. From Arizona's "Fathers Demanding Equal Justice" to "Fathers United for Equal Rights in Virginia,"[2] divorced men are banding together in most states to demand, among other things, a fairer chance at custody and stricter enforcement of part-time fathers' visitation rights and privileges.

The same groups of fathers are also trying to win the right to use the services of county attorneys free of charge to fine or punish wives who don't abide by visitation agreements. (Women, in some counties, can get free legal services to help them collect back alimony and child support.)

Making Visitation Work Better

Fortunately, most separated or divorced parents do see their children regularly (although two-thirds of the children of divorce as well as almost half of the children from intact families say they don't see their fathers *enough*). But even where there is regular contact, visitation can be trying and often frustrating. Being patient, having realistic goals, and keeping in mind a few points others have learned can help make it work better.

In order to avoid arguments with your former spouse, which can provoke him/her to become vindictive and make it difficult for you to see your children, establish a picking-up routine that will make the exchange of the children easy for their other parent to stick to. Be diligent about being on time yourself and about bringing them home when they're expected.

When it's your time to have your children, have them come to your house if they're old enough, or specify the time you will be picking them up and say that you'd like them to be ready when you arrive. If you must be in the house to see your children, for example if they are sick, avoid talking about sensitive subjects with your former spouse, such as how much you're going to contribute to fix the boiler, that you don't think your son should go to that expensive overnight camp, or whom either of you has been dating.

When children come to visit their other parent, they may not feel completely comfortable in the beginning. They may even say they don't want to go. What they usually really want is some extra coaxing to know you really want them. Having a room of their own or a corner of a room with a toy-box full of their things helps them to feel at home.

Learning the "Light Touch"

There are other typical dilemmas between the part-time parent and the visiting child. Nine-year-old Michael had a problem which many children of divorce face, perhaps because both parents and children are particularly sensitive to anything standing in the way of their limited time together. Yet, being sensitive to the other person's needs and flexible about occasional cancellations is the kind of understanding necessary to any close relationship.

"Tomorrow's Sunday, Mom, and the whole day is going to be ruined," he said to his mother.

"Why, Michael?"

"Because it's my day to see Dad and it's Neil's birthday party. I really want to go to the party but I know Dad will be angry and his feelings will be hurt and then I'll feel bad. Either way, the day will be ruined."

"Why don't you ask your father if you can see him Monday for dinner instead?" his mother suggested.

"Once I asked if we could change our day and he just said, 'Okay if you don't want to see me, Mike, let's just forget it,' and he hung up . . . Oh well, I'll try."

"Hello, Dad . . . Uh, do you think I could see you after school on Monday instead of tomorrow, just this one time?"

"Why, Mike?" asked his father.

"Well, it's Neil's birthday party tomorrow and I'd really like to go. But I want to see you too."

". . . Sure, Monday's fine. I'll pick you up at four-thirty. Have a good time at the party and tell me all about it, okay, son?" his father said.

"Oh, boy. Thanks, Dad. Thank you. Bye."

"Bye, Mike."

Some of the unhappiest moments between a child and a part-time parent can occur when the parent makes his child feel guilty or sorry for him if the child doesn't want to keep a date, not realizing as Michael's father did that it is normal and healthy for children to be attracted by birthday parties or backyard football games and that this in no way indicates a lack of feeling on the child's part. Saying "All right, if you don't want to see your own mother. I guess I'll manage" places too great a burden of guilt on a child.

"Don't let him know how much you need him," advises Dr. Sanger. On the other hand, if a child just says, "I don't know if I feel like going, Dad. Maybe I'll just stay home and play with my trains," you can insist and say, "Well, I really want to see *you* today and I'm sure we can find something fun to do," which shows a child you really care and that you're big enough to admit your feelings.

"Use a light touch and try to be flexible but not too casual with your child," says Dr. Sanger. Along this same line, there may be occasional times when a business or social appointment keeps you from seeing your child at a scheduled time. If you've shown him that you can adjust to a change in his plans once in a while, he will too. But don't make a habit of disappointing your child. And if you can't make it, give as much notice as possible. (Almost *nothing* makes him feel worse than his father not showing up.)

Don't Overdo It

Some new part-time parents spend all week trying to plan an exciting weekend for their children. But a veteran visiting parent says, "Try to keep your times with your child as normal as possible," . . . "Don't feel you have to make every Saturday a party." Occasional treats like the circus and a play are fine as special outings but they shouldn't happen regularly or children take them (and you) for granted.

Life is made up of walking, talking, cooking dinner, going to the supermarket, playing cards, reading books, and just being together, more than of carnivals, movies, and presents. Rather than buying your child a new toy each week, keep a couple of his favorite games at your home and take the time to play them with him, whether it's Monopoly, Scrabble, chess, or poker, and try to get involved in your son's or daughter's other interests—like looking through a microscope, making jewelry, cooking, bowling, or putting together model airplanes.

Indeed, many fathers and children find they have more fun together after the separation than they ever did before. Experts explain that fathers often relate to children *through* the children's mother or according to how well they, the fathers, are getting along with their wives. When their marriage deteriorates, often their relationship with their children does too. It is often calmer and happier after a separation.

Expecting Too Much

On the other hand, there are fathers who don't enjoy the time they spend with their children as much as they might because their expectations are too high.

"Some fathers feel guilty that their children don't have a full-time father," explains a psychologist. "They feel they're never doing enough and they try to pack too much into the times they spend with their children. If the child isn't completely thrilled with all the things his father does with him, the father is disappointed because he had unrealistic expectations for one day."

150

One father I talked with wondered why his twelve-year-old son, John, and ten-year-old daughter, Susan, had been balking so much about spending their usual visiting day with him.

What did he do with them, I asked. "Each week I have tickets for a concert or we go to one of the art museums," he explained to me. "I always wished someone had exposed me to those things earlier in my life and I know it's good for my children."

Again, a light touch is probably the best approach. While it may be admirable to dedicate yourself to the enrichment of your child's mind, if he is unhappy in the activity which you *insist* on, your time together will not go well. It really doesn't matter that museums may be "better" for your child than baseball games. As a father, while you should try to introduce your child to new and valuable experiences, presumably you also respect his tastes and try to please him. If you do so, he will probably be more open to your ideas.

How Much Discipline?

"Visiting" parents feel the time they spend with their children is so precious and meant to be enjoyed that they are often reluctant to discipline them. "I only see the girls twice a week," said one father, "and I want them to have a good time with me."

But this thinking creates a conflict that can ultimately be harmful to children. Not setting meal schedules or bedtime hours, feeding a child sweets instead of meat and vegetables, and not instituting other rules of behavior can create monsters who will be difficult to handle when they get home and who will legitimately anger the parent who has to cope with them. This can kindle some of the old conflicts that had everyone in a state of tension before the divorce. And children will eventually resent a parent's laxity because they know discipline is a form of caring.

It is fair to expect a parent to set standards for his children when they visit, but it is not fair to expect those children to be completely calm when they return from a day or weekend with their part-time parent. A child in that situation *normally* will be excited, overly active and less able to control himself than usual. A parent should guard against interpreting her child's excited state as meaning that the child didn't enjoy the visit or that it wasn't good for him.

On the other hand and for the very reason that a visit to a parent can be extremely exciting, a part-time parent should see to it that the child goes to bed at a reasonable hour if he is spending the night or that he arrives home in time to get a good night's sleep, *particularly* on school nights.

Teachers and school directors have described a "Monday morning syndrome" in children who have spent the preceding Sunday or weekend with the parent they don't live with. "They're usually tired. They might be whiny, excitable, unable to concentrate, or a little withdrawn. It usually takes at least until Tuesday before they're themselves again," reported one nursery school director.

Keeping in Touch When You're Apart

As a part-time parent, what you do when you're not with your child is important to him too. When you leave him, let him know when you'll be seeing him next. Write letters or notes even if you live nearby. Call your child on the phone. Ask about school, his friends, his hobbies, movies he's seen, what he wants to be, or anything else that builds rapport and closeness.

Discuss his feelings once in a while too, how he feels now that you and his mother have separated. Ask him how he thinks you're doing as a father. You might be pleasantly surprised by his answer or you may get some helpful suggestions, but it's important to keep the lines of communication open. Give him telephone numbers where he can reach you and let him know it's okay for him to call you.

Since you don't see your child every day, when you buy him a present try to select something special. "The best gifts I bought my daughter, I think, were a poster to hang on her wall, a little pocketbook to carry with her, and a shirt with her name on the front. She picked them out and I thought they were good because they would last and they would make her think of me," said one father.

The Indifferent Parent

There are difficulties and challenges for the visiting parent who *wants* to see his child, but what about the parent who seems indifferent and who doesn't bother much with his or her child?

"First of all, make up a visiting schedule that makes it as easy as possible for the other parent to see the child," says one psychiatrist, who feels that one parent often loses interest because the other parent sets so many rules and conditions ("Sorry, you weren't here by ten o'clock. Jennifer can't see you today") that they give up. Every-

153

thing should be done, including suggesting counseling to an uncooperative parent, to see to it that a child gets to see both parents regularly.

If, however, a parent really drops out of a child's life—moves to another state, remarries, and sends only a Christmas card to acknowledge his child, or simply just becomes too busy to be involved on a regular basis—what should a child's custodial parent do to make the situation easier for the child to deal with?

"Explain to the child that there's something not right about his parent that makes him not care about his own child. Emphasize that it's the parent's problem, and it's *not* the child's fault. He's not unlovable because his father doesn't show he loves him," advises a psychiatrist. "But it's easier said than done. It's still going to hurt. You must give the child as much chance as possible to form meaningful attachments to other relatives, teachers, and friends of the same sex as the parent he doesn't see. This child may have trouble with his self-esteem. He should have some counseling or therapy if he seems to be falling down in school, not making friends, or behaving as though he doesn't value himself. Talking out his feelings always helps but professional help—at least a consultation—may be wise."

How the Part-Time Parent Feels

Therapists explain that parents themselves, particularly fathers, often benefit from counseling to help them adjust to being out of their homes, separated from their wives and apart from their children . . . As one woman put it, "My husband is having a tougher time of it out there. I have my problems, sure, but in some ways I can see that it's harder on him. It's very important to him that he has the kids even for one or two days a week."

One of the greatest fears of the part-time father is fear that he will be replaced by someone else, that he will become a fuzzy memory, or worse, a relatively unimportant casual visitor. Sam explained how he felt one Sunday afternoon while he was walking with his ten-year-old son, Brandon, who casually said, "I'm lucky, Dad, you know why?"

"Why, son?" Sam asked.

"Because George plays a lot more baseball with me than you did when you lived with us."

"I felt something grab me in my throat and my stomach and the tears were ready," said Sam, "But I was proud of myself for saying, 'Good, Brandy, I'm glad George is nice to you and that you have someone to play baseball with.' I'm lucky I live nearby; otherwise I'd be worried that I couldn't hang on to him," Sam said, "and that's why I spend all my vacations with him. Sure, once in a while I'd like to do something else. But you can't hang on to your kids without putting in the time and the work."

The life of a part-time parent—seeing your children by appointment, being outside their day-to-day lives—can be painful and lonely at times. But, being a good part-time parent can be invaluable to your children. And to you.

Your influence will increase their sense of security and self-esteem and will surely help to shape the kinds of people they become. From the standpoint of your own needs, raising children is, according to many people, the most creatively rich experience there is and, even on a part-time basis, can add so much to your sense of well-being. (As for part-time vs. full-time, one divorced father who sees his children Wednesday afternoons and evenings and at least half of every weekend says, "I spend at least as much time with my children now as I did before my separation. Without the children's mother here to do things for them and make most of the decisions, our time together is probably more meaningful than it was before when I was physically around more but actually less involved.")

Your "visiting" relationship with your children may seem limited while they are young, but many parents say that as their children get older, relationships become closer. Some have even found that their older children eventually asked to come and live with them.

"Your relationship with your child is for life," commented one father. "I almost made the mistake of letting mine slip away after my separation because I was angry at my ex-wife; my son was being difficult and I didn't want to deal with the situation. But I hung in and my son and I are very close now."

PART THREE

SPECIAL CUSTODY SITUATIONS

Chapter Twelve

THE HOMOSEXUAL PARENT AND CUSTODY

A Contradiction?

Lesbian mothers? Gay fathers? In what may sound like a contradiction in terms, some writers have explained that only after years of marriage do some men and women become aware of their homosexual tendencies. Still others, they say, reject the gay life for a time in favor of marriage and a family. Some hope they will become more comfortable as heterosexuals, others primarily want to have children.

Gary, a man whose thick blond hair, sky-blue eyes and tall, lanky body belied his thirty-nine years but not his past as both a basketball and tennis star in college, is a case in point. Gary was also a Phi Beta Kappa with highest honors in mathematics who was in demand by several top universities as soon as he had finished his

Ph.D. work. By the time he had completed his doctorate, he and his wife had two children and his wife had started medical school. This monopolized most of her days and evenings for classes and library work as well as a good number of nights and weekends for required hospital work. During his wife's hectic seven years of medical school, internship, and residency, Gary's teaching and research schedule allowed him to spend some afternoons, most evenings, and most weekends with his children. He was their primary parent. Among his favorite times with his children, he said, were "playing the piano for them and teaching them to play, and reading Tolkien's *Lord of the Rings* again and again."

To anyone who had known Gary as a parent, it would probably have come as a surprise that when he and his wife divorced some time later, he was told by his lawyer that he wouldn't "have a chance in hell" at winning custody of his children. And indeed the court even granted him less visitation time with his children than is customary.

This unusual turn of events came about, Gary explains (and the court records substantiate) because at around the age of thirty-two, he openly admitted what he secretly had felt for years—that he was a homosexual.

"When I was fifteen, I went to our minister and told him I thought I had a problem. I told him I was attracted to guys.

"He started yelling at me," Gary went on, "and saying, 'You're no queer. Those guys run around in dresses. You don't want to be like that, do you?' I said, No I didn't. And he said, 'Think of what it would do to your mother and father.' He told me to forget about it and go out with girls, which I did.

"During my second year of college," he continued, "I

went to talk to a psychiatrist and he told me pretty much the same thing. He said everyone goes through times when they may doubt themselves. He said I was a jock, a top student, and could have my pick of girls. He advised me to continue dating girls and said that I'd probably marry and have children and look back on this time and laugh."

Gary did marry—the homecoming queen—and have children, but he never looked back and laughed. "When I was twenty-nine, I had my first homosexual experience. I never told anyone because I loved my kids and had too many responsibilities. A couple of years later, my wife told me she wanted a divorce. She soon married another man.

"She had custody of the children initially but I planned to try to get them. But when she learned that I was gay, she was repelled. She went to court saying that I shouldn't see the children as much as I had. The judge ended up ruling that I could no longer keep the children overnight when they visited on weekends, but he said that they could spend a month in the summer with me. Figure out the logic in that."

The judge in Gary's case also ruled that at no time during the children's visits was Gary to have a man with whom he was sexually involved in his home.

With encouragement to be true to oneself coming from both the feminist and the gay-rights movements, it is not so surprising that many men and women who are "coming out" today were formerly married and have children. (It has been estimated by many authorities that approximately 10 percent of the population is primarily homosexual. Among lesbians, experts say, 13–20 percent are mothers.)

Their children must deal not only with their parents' divorce but with the fact that one of their parents is a homosexual.

Does a Homosexual Parent Affect a Child's Development?

The concern of this book has been to try to point out and defend what is best for the child where custody and visitation are at issue. Where there is a homosexual parent involved, this concern must include the questions: Does living with a homosexual parent increase the probability that a child will become homosexual? What effects would living with a homosexual parent (full- or part-time) be likely to have on a child's development? Is there valid reason to interfere in the relationship between parent and child on the basis of a parent's homosexuality, as many courts and nongay parents have done? These are some of the questions which this chapter will address.

The basic causes of homosexuality, while not fully understood, are believed by one of the country's leading sex researchers to be rooted not in the sexual orientations of a child's parents but rather in some serious emotional disturbance in the child's early life which occurred well before such things are even understood on a conscious level—between the ages of eighteen months and four and a half years. This upsetting experience, according to this theory, disrupts and confuses a child's normal development, specifically his gender orientation at the most critical time. "The emotional disruption may be far removed from anything to do with sex or with having a feminine mother and a masculine father," says Dr. John

162

Money, Professor of Medical Psychology, Psychiatry, and Pediatrics at The Johns Hopkins University School of Medicine. "It could be something as unrelated as having a grandfather living with the family who is in an oxygen tent where the parents are continually preoccupied, depressed, and concerned that the last heart attack is coming."

Other psychiatrists feel that part of the explanation for homosexuality is what is called "modeling" theory, that children imitate and model their behavior after those around them and therefore could "learn" homosexuality by imitation.

Most experts, however, now feel modeling theory is too simplistic an explanation for the origins of homosexuality, some pointing out as Dr. Benjamin Spock does, that "most homosexuals are the children of conventionally heterosexual parents."

In fact, the varied and complex causes of homosexuality have not been proven to anyone's complete satisfaction. Yet custody and visitation decisions concerning children with homosexual parents must be made today and every day and must be based on the latest, albeit imperfect, understandings.

Not only are there varying opinions on the causes of homosexuality, but the psychiatric community is also in disagreement over whether homosexuality is an illness (some distinguished members are convinced that it is a developmental illness related to some form of emotional deprivation by a parent; other prominent experts say they feel it is a more normal variation).

It follows logically that since experts disagree on the *causes* of homosexuality and whether or not it is a form of mental illness, there would be further debate and disagreement as to the *effects* which a homosexual parent might have on a child's sexual orientation and emotional well-being.

Yet, virtually no medical or psychological experts with whom I spoke felt that a person's homosexuality, *per se*, was reason to deny custody or curtail visitation. "Each case should be judged individually and on many factors," says Dr. Kestenbaum. Those many factors should add up to the best interests of the child with parents being judged on the basis of their love, devotion, and ability to care for their children; their character; their integrity; their reliability; their optimism; and their stability.

Dr. Wardell Pomeroy, long-time associate of and co-author with the late Alfred Kinsey, states, "There is no evidence to my knowledge that children of homosexual parents are themselves more likely to become homosexual. Very often," he cautions, "the parent who has the children tries to prohibit the other parent from seeing them, not because of their homosexuality, but because they are . . . using the homosexual issue as an excuse."

Yet, while society has become more sensitive to the problems and civil rights of homosexuals, few authorities would go so far as to say, as some gay-rights advocates have done, that a parent's sexual orientation is a neutral issue. Most agree that children of all ages benefit from role models of the same sex. However, most also separate a person's private sexual behavior from his ability to be a parent. A person's sexual life is his own business, they say, but how sensitive he is to his child's needs in the *acting out of his sexual life* is a factor which does affect his qualifications as a parent.

"A prostitute who goes to her place of work at 9:00 A.M., returns home at 5:30 P.M. and provides a stable, loving home for a child is quite different from one who does her work in her home and exposes her child to a sleazy environment," says Dr. Money.

Similarly, "a home that is strewn with gay pornographic literature or one that is a thoroughfare for a parade of lovers is destructive to a child's sense of security and is flagrantly abusive of a child's needs," Dr. Kestenbaum points out and goes on to say that similar promiscuity among heterosexuals would be equally upsetting to a child. The point is that some authorities have found homosexuals to be, on the average, more promiscuous than heterosexuals.

While children don't simply "learn" their sexual preference, and while a child's basic gender orientation is believed to be established before the age of five, some psychiatrists feel that the environment provided for youngsters during their pre-teen and teen-age years can have a significant impact on, among other things, sexual behavior. Some adolescents, particularly those whose self-confidence is not as strong as others and who might therefore be more easily led, will be more in need of attention, they say, and could be adversely influenced if they were regularly in a homosexual milieu.

As a teen-ager struggles to affirm his heterosexuality and develop relationships with the opposite sex, "he must have the ego strength to accept a lot of rejection and frustration," says child psychiatrist Richard Gardner. "Most girls whom a teen-age boy approaches will probably not respond to him, so he has to be able to take the rejection," says Gardner. "Then, even if a girl does show interest, sexual gratification will take time and the boy has to be able to take the frustration.

"If you put that boy in a homosexual environment where he will be very attractive to a number of men and where sexual gratification can be immediate, at the very least you may cause him severe anxiety and titillation, followed by guilt and confusion."

Other experts caution against becoming obsessed with the influence of one parent on a child, pointing out that children usually have many role models with whom to identify—brothers, sisters, teachers and friends—as well as parents. Yet a good number of children whose parents are divorced may not have any other role models than their parents. They may have moved and not have many friends or be only children.

On the question of parental influence, "Young children also learn gender identity from the *opposite* sex," says Dr. Money. "In other words, boys learn to become masculine from seeing masculine behavior, but also from being praised and encouraged by their mothers."

A frequent objection to children being in the custody of homosexual parents is that others will probably learn about their parent's homosexuality and they will be ridiculed by their peers, as children often are who are different. Dr. Marmor argues, "Difference is not easily accepted in our culture, but it is a fact of life. Just as intelligent black or Jewish parents can help their children to cope with bigotry, so can homosexual parents." However, helping children to cope with homosexual parents would involve detailed discussions of sexuality which could be unsettling to children. No such comparable discussion would go with the problems of racial or religious bigotry.

While most psychologists and psychiatrists feel that we don't know enough at this point to understand both the short and the long-range effects of living part-time or full-time with a homosexual parent, we do know something else which may be the most important consideration. "Above all, it is important that a child of divorce be able to

166

preserve a good quality relationship with both the father and the mother," says Dr. Money. "It is the caliber of the parent and parenthood that counts, not the sex or eroticism of the parent's friend or partner."

A child of divorce both of whose parents maintain a close relationship with him has the best chance of a healthy adjustment. Most child experts seldom *recommend* custody for a homosexual parent. But they are reluctant to compromise on the principle of both parents remaining involved with a child, except in cases where the child is in clear physical or emotional danger. They seem to feel that this is generally not the case with homosexual parents.

Where the Courts Stand

The courts, on the other hand, have varied greatly in their decisions on custody and visitation rights of homosexual parents. Some judges look primarily at the stability of the home. Others say homosexuality is reason enough to render a parent unfit. There have been many cases where the issue of homosexuality has controlled the decision. A good number of those cases, experts say, have not been in the best interests of the children.

The trial experiences of two Washington women illustrate the unpredictable influence which homosexuality can have.

According to the social worker's report, "Both Nancy —
—— and Marilyn —— are mature, responsible individuals with very adequate parenting skills. Both Nancy ——
— and Marilyn —— use discretion regarding their sexual relationship, considering this but one aspect of an overall mutual friendship."

In Nancy's case, the judge awarded her custody of her

children after being convinced that she was a good parent and that her relationship with Marilyn was a stable one.

A different judge took away custody of two of Marilyn's three children. Disregarding the children's pleas to remain with their mother as well as unanimous expert opinion from a psychiatrist, a psychologist, and a social worker to the effect that the mother should have custody, the judge feared that the women's lesbian relationship would harm the children. When the ten- and twelve-year-old children ran away from the father's home, the judge stood firm in his belief that "the living arrangement of their mother is an abnormal and not a stable one . . ." and that because the father would refuse to visit the children if they were in the mother's custody, it would not be in the children's best interests to live with their mother.

After being temporarily placed in a juvenile detention center, the children were later assigned permanently to a married half-sister.[1]

In another case a couple was divorced after seven years of marriage, with a girl, six, and boy, two. The father had denied that he was the father of the younger child, did not want custody of the children, moved seventy miles away after the divorce, and soon remarried. Both wives had sought police protection following incidents of his hitting them. Within six months of the divorce, his support payments to his ex-wife and children had stopped.

Three years later, when the father learned that his former wife had another woman living with her with whom she had a lesbian relationship, he became livid. He sued for custody, saying he was "a real man and could offer the children a stable home."

In the judge's chambers, the nine-year-old said she wanted to live only with her mother as did her five-year-old brother who had not seen his father more than a half-dozen times during his life. Teachers claimed the children were well-adjusted. Neighbors reported that the mother met the children's school bus every day and often had the children's friends at her house to play. Two psychiatrists testified that the mother was a loving, stable person whom the children loved and with whom they were functioning well, while the father had neglected the children before as well as after the divorce and was an unstable personality.

The judge awarded custody to the father.

Telling the Children

Many lesbian and gay parents afraid of jeopardizing their custody or visitation rights wonder whether to tell their children about their homosexuality. Others are concerned that they might influence their children's sexual tendencies by telling them.

"I don't know what to do," said a nurse. "If I tell them, what will they think of me? They'll probably say I'm repulsive. I don't want to hurt them . . . or myself."

"It's better that they know about it," says Dr. Kestenbaum. "It's a reality issue."

Dr. Levy's advice "Give children the truth and they can deal with it" applies as well here as in other areas of childrearing. It is almost impossible to keep something so major a secret from a child anyway, and if he senses a conspiracy, it may play havoc with his fantasies. And learning it from someone else without being prepared, or

169

asking you about it at an inopportune or embarrassing moment can create an ugly, unforgettable scene.

Deciding that you should tell your child about this part of your life is not enough. Planning what to say and being prepared for their reactions are equally important.

Experts advise you to plan ahead of time what you want to say to your children ("I have something I want you to know that's important to you and me"), bring them together in a quiet place, or if there's a large age difference, tell them separately. Be prepared for the intense pain and shock they are likely to feel when you tell them.

"You queer!"

"Dyke!"

Your children may react harshly at first—they're feeling a combination of shock, embarrassment, and worry over how this will directly affect them.

They will want to know if your being gay means that they will be too. Tell them that while you have found this to be right and most comfortable for you, they won't be because you are. They have had different experiences and they have a different makeup than you do.

Dr. Money points out that responsible parents should go further. They should interpret society accurately to their children, he says, and feels it is only fair to include in an explanation of a parent's homosexuality that being gay is not what the large majority of people are nor what society values, so that while it's not something to be ashamed of, neither is it a way of life to aspire to.

In discussing the subject with your children, it is very important that children of the opposite sex, whether they come out and ask it or not, be reassured that even though you prefer a person of the same sex, you do not dislike their sex or them.

170

How do the children themselves see this issue? One sixteen-year-old boy, who dates girls regularly, when asked about his gay father with whom he spends alternate weekends, said, "My dad is a good guy. I wish he were straight like my friends' fathers, but I'm glad for him that he's happier this way."

A young teen-age girl, who lives with her lesbian mother and the mother's lover and does not see her father, was asked whether she thought she would be a lesbian. "Probably," the girl answered.

The fairest plea to parents and judges who are intimately involved in custody and visitation decisions between children and homosexual parents must be to take the most painstaking care in evaluating the characters of the parents involved and the needs and wishes of their children.

Chapter Thirteen

GRANDPARENTS AND CUSTODY

Grandparents with Custody

Now that the best interests of the child is the standard that usually prevails in custody matters, grandparents, being as close as they often are to their grandchildren, occasionally win full custody of those children.

In one such case, the mother of eight-year-old Katie had died. After her father remarried about a year later, the child spent many weekends and vacations with her grandmother. When Katie's new stepmother later gave birth to twin girls, Katie was being brought to her grandmother's on an ever more frequent basis, sometimes even spending several weeks at a time there. Finally, her grandmother, with the child's encouragement, decided to seek custody.

After a long, complex case in which the judge was torn

between the child's interests and her father's right to custody, he ruled that Katie, an articulate ten-year-old who was firm in her desire to live with her grandmother, would be in custody of the grandmother and that her father would have liberal visiting time.

Then there are those grandparents who do not have official custody of their grandchildren following the marital breakup of one of their children but who end up with much of the day-to-day responsibility for them.

"My daughter went back to work and asked me to take care of the children. Of course, I love them, but at times it's too much for me and I resent it" is the way one grandmother explained her predicament. "And I'm not sure it's so good for them either," she went on. "I don't have the strength to take care of their physical needs *and* discipline them. So they're pretty spoiled."

Grandparents As Caretakers

Women who go back to work following their separation and cannot afford full-time help often move in with their mothers or fathers or ask them to take care of the children while they, the mothers, work. This can cause confusion in a child as to who has the authority and it may lead to a situation where a grown daughter allows herself and her child to be taken care of by her mother. While older parents can offer temporary comfort after a separation, regression on the part of the younger parent to a dependent mother-daughter situation will not be helpful to anyone's long-range growth and healthy adjustment.

174

Grandparents, Keep Out!

Divorce can sever more than the link between husband and wife. It can cut grandchildren off from grandparents and children off from their roots.

Paternal grandparents are the ones most likely to find themselves out of touch, denied access to their grandchildren. The grandchildren, in turn, who had previously enjoyed the unqualified, doting kind of love that only comes from grandmothers and grandfathers may no longer be permitted to see them, to receive letters and packages from them, or to speak to them on the telephone. They may try to get in touch with their grandparents secretly. Often they become depressed and fall behind in school.

Why? Because one of their parents stands between them and their grandparents, usually a mother who feels her in-laws interfered too much in her marriage, one who wants to get on with her new life with as few reminders of the past as possible, or one whose limited communication with her in-laws ended with the marriage.

The last situation happened in the case of Bess and Jason, two children who lived in Philadelphia and had grandparents in Massachusetts.

"Every summer the children used to spend August with us on the Cape," Bess and Jason's grandmother explained, "and we would go to their home for two weeks at Christmas. Now our cards, letters and presents come back to us unopened. We haven't even talked to the children in nine months."

In the standoff between the generations, the biggest losers are the children. In many instances, where they

175

had been deeply attached to their grandparents, they suffer a severe loss, one almost equivalent to the death of a grandparent and far more confusing.

Some grandparents, though, are determined not to accept this fate. By going through the courts, going to counselors, and by organizing to gain political strength, many are fighting to change a far too common and cruel occurrence.

One activist grandmother, fifty-five-year-old Luella Davison from Sylvan Lake, Michigan, two years ago formed an organization called Grandparents Anonymous. Mrs. Davison explains that when she heard the stories of so many others, she was doubly convinced of the grief involved when grandparents and grandchildren are separated. "It's like a death to both parties—the grandparents and grandchildren . . . But our first concern is with the grandchildren."

While progress is slow for Grandparents Anonymous and the few similar groups that exist, they lend much-needed support to their members and lobby to further legislation on grandparents' rights to visit their grandchildren regardless of the marital status of the children's parents.

In the eyes of the law, grandparents have been making some inroads. New York, Delaware, Ohio, Virginia, Georgia, Illinois, Iowa, Kansas, California, Arkansas, Kentucky, Louisiana, Missouri, New Jersey, Oklahoma, Tennessee, Texas, Utah, Wisconsin, and Minnesota have enacted some degree of protection by law of grandparents' visitation rights. Mrs. Davison's home state of Michigan has a bill sponsored by Representative William Jowett currently before the legislature. Where only a short time ago grandparents had no legal right to petition for visitation except if their own children had died, in many states they now may go through the courts and present their case for seeing their grandchildren on a regular basis.

Some family counselors, social workers, and psychologists have succeeded in blunting the resistance of daughters- or sons-in-law to their children seeing their grandparents by using counseling to stress what they feel is the key point—that in most cases the children are being used and deprived because of differences between adults. They also explain that children's lives are enriched by having close, loving relationships with their grandparents, especially in a time when more mothers and fathers work and families move so frequently that they lose touch with their own histories. Where families are further split apart by divorce, grandparents can provide a sense of stability and continuity. Only a grandma or grandpa can offer the deep satisfaction to a child that comes with stories beginning, "When your Mommy was a little girl," or "When your Daddy was a little boy . . ."

Mrs. Davison urges any grandparents who feel they are being fully or partially denied visitation with their grandchildren to "write and visit state senators and representatives. Tell them your personal story," she says.

The Role of Relatives

Most often, grandparents and other relatives react similarly to a separation in the family. While they worry about the children and how everyone will manage in what is to most of them the strange, adverse climate of divorce, they usually try to be supportive and commonly offer to spend time with the children or to give financial assistance.

Yet occasionally, relatives can·contribute to destructive outcomes. Because of their dislike for a son- or daughter-in-law or their willingness to help their child punish his or her former spouse, they can lose sight of the price the children will pay for their elders' revenge.

"I knew one mother who took her five-year-old child to Europe where the child's father couldn't find them," explains one attorney. "Her wealthy parents gave her whatever money she wanted and she lived in several different places for a period of about four years."

"The child has been lied to, tricked, confused, told that his father is no good, and by now he's probably not sure of who his father is or what he is like," said a psychiatrist. "The effects on the child are terribly destructive."

For the sake of children, it is best if mothers, fathers, and grandparents try not to find fault or fix blame on anyone for a divorce. Where everyone concentrates on keeping up a loving relationship with the children, everyone will be better off. Grandparents can play an important part in giving children love and support at this time—provided they recognize how important it is not to add any more conflict to the family and provided the grandchildren's parents allow grandparents to be involved.

Chapter Fourteen

CUSTODY AND THE HANDICAPPED CHILD

Johanna and Richard married in 1966 during Richard's year as an intern at a Washington, D.C., hospital. At that time, Johanna had been teaching English for two years in a suburban high school.

While she continued working, Richard completed his internship and a three-year residency in pediatrics. Because he had been given a deferment by the army in order to complete his education in exchange for agreeing to serve as a physician for two years after he finished, he and Johanna soon were headed for an army base in southern Texas.

With a major's salary as income and relatively low living expenses Richard and Johanna decided that she would not work but would try to start a family. Less than a year later, Kirsten was born and two-and-a-half years after that, after the family had relocated in Houston, Alexander came along.

It would have been the perfect "millionaire's split"—a boy and a girl. Except that Alexander was found to be retarded. Judging from tests they performed, the doctors said that his retardation was not severe. He would be able to attend school at some point and learn some basic skills.

But that verdict was not enough and at the same time it was too much for Richard. He was angry, depressed, not coping well with what psychiatrists would call a narcissistic injury—something so close and so painful that one can only pull back from it. The reality that his child would never be normal was too powerful for him to deal with. Through it all, Johanna tried to be positive and make the best of things.

Richard knew that each day the gap between Alexander and the other children would widen. As this proceeded to happen over the next two years, the marriage deteriorated. Richard withdrew, working more and spending less time at home.

One day he announced that he was accepting a position at a hospital and medical school back in Washington. He said he felt that he and Johanna should separate and that he wanted to take Kirsten but felt that Johanna could handle Alexander ever so much better than he.

Johanna was close to immobilized by the intensity of her emotions. She adored Kirsten and knew that the child was closest to her and would suffer from this move. Yet she didn't think she could take on the financial costs of a custody battle. She also knew that she would need every bit of Richard's support for the costly special schools and health care which Alexander would need. Four weeks later, Richard and four-and-a-half-year-old Kirsten were on their way to Washington.

Over the course of the next several years, Richard saw Alexander once and sent him two birthday cards. Johanna eventually moved to Washington in order to be closer to Kirsten, but soon after that, Richard went on to New York with his daughter. Not only did he not want to see Alexander, but he tried to discourage Kirsten's relationship with the boy.

Richard's and Johanna's case is one of thousands of some of the most tragic custody situations, those involving handicapped children. With the additional strains involved, parents of handicapped children face greater possibilities of marital difficulties and, if and when they separate, more difficulty managing custody. Unfortunately, many children and parents are cruelly hurt in one of the unfairest of circumstances. While educational programs for the handicapped have progressed a great deal over the past several years, it seems that the problem of single parents with handicapped children should be more specifically addressed and calls for, when there is no other recourse, government programs and assistance.

PART FOUR

BEFORE AND AFTER THE CUSTODY AGREEMENT

Chapter Fifteen

HOW TO PREPARE THE CHILDREN

At the news of a separation, children not only ask "why?" but may demand to know, "Why didn't you tell us sooner?"

Some parents who sense that their marriages are failing mistakenly try to conceal the signals from their children—the arguments, the sarcasm, the silence—until one day, Daddy is packing his suitcases or Mommy is whisking them back home to her parents or off to a different apartment. These parents are missing an important opportunity to help their children make sense of and accept the separation.

Preparing children for the family breakup may be among the most painful tasks of a lifetime. But parents must do it and it is much more than a matter of breaking the bad news.

Some parents feel that the fact that their children have

witnessed fights, heard their parents shout, seen them cry is preparation enough. It is not. Children need to be prepared, with preventive measures, to be able to handle crisis. This means that parents must see that children have plenty of chances to express their grief, to relieve some of their inevitable guilt, and to ask questions.

Unlike some adults who take divorce more or less in stride or even look forward to it (like the woman who told me, "At last I'm legally separated, now my life can begin"), children almost never feel this way. Given their choice, most would probably prefer an unhappy family, something they know, to a divorce—an unknown and therefore frightening change.

The weeks or months before the separation give parents not-to-be-missed opportunities to prepare children for the stress that is to come and for the custody arrangement which will be the framework of their new lives.

Why You Must Prepare the Children

For most children, parental separation is their first life-crisis, or in the words of child psychiatrist Sirgay Sanger, "their first experience with the unthinkable." Sanger and others feel exposing children to controlled amounts of frustrating and "unthinkable" experiences in their daily lives strengthens them for any stresses they will face, including separation should it happen.

Psychiatrist Gilbert Kliman, who, as the Director for the Center for Preventive Psychiatry in White Plains, New York, is accustomed to seeing children overwhelmed by family crises, is also convinced that much childhood trauma can be avoided. He advises *all* parents to provide children with "small doses of stress." This is easy enough to provide in everyday life. It is a matter of putting the children in touch with reality; being truthful, for instance, about a parent who has a drinking problem or a grandmother who is seriously ill. Don't conceal the fact that Daddy has been fired or that the family cat was run over.

Coping is, for the most part, learned behavior. A child will deal with separation in a way that reflects how his parents handle stressful situations, and particularly how they are dealing with the separation themselves.

If parents face stress honestly and rationally ("This is going to be hard, but we can handle it"), they are teaching their children a healthy, mature approach. It is a mistake to mislead children about stress-provoking situations. If you tell them the truth and explain what it will mean to them, they learn to cope more competently than most parents expect.

If, on the other hand, parents hide the truth about a divorce or other crisis (and the children will most probably sense the deception anyway), they give the children a weakening, frightening message—that stress is a part of life to be denied, feared, repressed, whispered about, swept under the rug, run away from.

The parents who say "Let's not tell Billy about the separation until the summer. We'll say you're traveling on business" are almost certainly hurting their child. Billy's fantasies are probably far worse than the truth ("Maybe Daddy's never coming back"). He may be confused and feeling guilty about why daddy left ("I'm dumb. That's why Daddy went away"). They have deprived Billy of an important chance to learn to cope with stress. When parents cover up or distort reality, children usually fantasize even more frightening "realities." When parents panic in difficult situations, their children will learn the same feelings of inadequacy. One early result of these disturbing fantasies and anxieties is an inability to concentrate and study in school, which can lead to serious learning problems.

Child psychiatrist Sanger suggests that parents help children deal with "unthinkables," such as separation, by developing a "vocabulary of the inner life." For instance, talk with your child occasionally about stressful things that are happening right in his life, such as "It must be a little scary for Matthew to have to go to the hospital. How do you think he was feeling when he went to have his tonsils out?"

Or, "How do you think Mary and Kirk are feeling now that their parents aren't living together anymore? . . . How often do they see their father? . . . What do they do with him? . . . It seems as though they get to be with him quite a lot" helps a child to identify with the idea.

Doll play can be helpful, too. Pointing to a doll and saying "This little girl is lost. How do you think she is feeling?" introduces a child to anxiety, fear, and loss in a way that he or she can handle. One psychiatrist suggests that parents think of it as immunizing a child against stressful emotions. They may experience the emotion, but it won't devastate them. Again, make these talks *occasional*, not frequent, and only where they come up naturally in conversation. You don't want your child preoccupied with divorce, death, and surgery.

Once parents foresee an imminent separation, they should introduce that fact in a gentle, gradual way to their children. When there has been an argument, say something about it, perhaps "Daddy and Mommy surely got each other upset today. You might have been upset too. It's hard for everybody when we argue." At a later time, you might even say, "Mommy and Daddy don't seem to be able to live in the same house very happily" or "Daddy hasn't been home much because we haven't been getting along."

Ian and Dorothy's parents argued frequently. One evening, their mother, Jeanette, said to the two children at bedtime, "It seems as though Daddy and Mommy don't get along very well lately, doesn't it? We're sorry about all this fighting."

"Why *do* you fight so much?" Dorothy asked quickly, sounding thankful for the opportunity.

"We can't seem to agree about a lot of things, sweetheart," explained their mother, "and we don't make each other happy."

Ian and Dorothy said nothing further on the subject that night, but with that brief conversation, their mother had freed them from their isolation and their pretenses. She let them know they could ask any questions they had. Where children don't have a chance to ask questions and air their feelings, their concerns won't disappear, but may go underground and take the form of disturbed behavior.

In mid-July, on a summer weekend at their lake house, Marilyn gave Bob her reasons for wanting a separation. She explained that because of the years of arguments and tension, and Bob's unwillingness to talk to a counselor with her, she had decided that there was no hope that things would improve. She said she would start looking for a job in the city immediately and would plan to live with Jessie in their city apartment after the summer.

Because Bob traveled extensively in his job, he was rarely at their apartment. Following the talk she had with Bob, Marilyn began to drive the forty miles to the city every week to look for a job, leaving five-year-old Jessie with their mother's helper at the lake for periods of three to five days. Neither parent told Jessie what was going on.

The strange thing to Jessie was that her mother was seldom with her at the lake and was never there on weekends when her father came. On the rare occasions when Jessie asked her father about it, he covered up with answers like "Oh, you know Mommy's been looking for a job in the city. She just doesn't have much time right now."

One day two friends of Jessie's asked her where her mother was. "Mommy is working in the city," Jessie snapped. "She has an important job and she even has to work on Saturdays and Sundays, *and don't ask me any more about it!*"

By the end of the summer, when Marilyn, Jessie, and the mother's helper were packing to move back to the city, the child still hadn't been told about the separation. She had become belligerent, often shrieked and screamed at her mother and friends, and one evening, as she had on many other occasions, Jessie stomped off in sobs after a disagreement over who would go first in Parcheesi.

Had Marilyn and Bob been frank with Jessie, it would have served two important purposes and while it may have been agonizing at the time, in the long run, it would have made the child healthier. *First,* frankness clarifies the situation, relieving a child of many confusions or fantasies which he is probably harboring. He or she needs to know *exactly* what his parents are doing and why they are doing it, because this will affect the child very directly. Most importantly, he needs to know about himself and his future—whom he will be with, where he will live, how often he will see his other parent?

190

Second, being honest with a child reinforces his somewhat shaken trust in his parents and makes other things they are going to say more believable. If they haven't leveled with a child, he may not believe them when they promise "We will always love you and take care of you in spite of the separation," while if he believes they're straight with him, he will feel more secure about his future.

Frankness with children about a separation, experts say, should include an explanation, in as dignified a way as possible, of the *reasons* for the separation. If Mommy loves someone else or Daddy has a problem which makes him drink too much, explain this to them—sensitively. It is easier for children to come to grips with the truth than with secrecy and distortions.

What to Tell the Children

When explaining a separation to children, try to: (1) help them understand the reasons for it, perhaps explaining that it's not something you decided suddenly or without trying hard to work things out but, on the other hand, don't stress the sexual aspects. This may lead to areas children are too young to understand. Point out to them that while this upsets them, you were extremely unhappy with things as they had been and that it's not good for anyone in the family if (Mommy) (Daddy) is sad, and; (2) reassure them about their future (again, whom they will live with, where they'll live, how much and when they will see their other parent); (3) Try to be optimistic. "We'll manage. There won't be as much fighting. We'll all feel more relaxed. One or both of us may get married again someday."

191

Linda and David told their children about their impending separation one evening after dinner. "Children, come down here, will you?" David called.

Luke bounded down the stairs, dropping his husky, six-year-old body into the deep cushions of the couch. Molly, eleven, with the posture of a third-year ballet student, walked into the living room, sat down in a wing chair and continued reading her book.

Their mother began, "Children, Daddy and I have something important to tell you . . . It's something that will be hard for you to understand . . . First, we want both of you to know how much we love you and that we will always take care of you. That will never, ever change." By this time, the two children were staring at their parents.

"Mommy and I are getting a separation," David said. "As you both know, we haven't been getting along very well. We've tried to work things out but they aren't getting better. Your mother and I are going to try living in different places. We'll both be with you a lot but you will live here with Mommy and go to your regular school every day. I'll be living in an apartment in Brookfield Gardens. It's less than ten minutes away and you can ride your bikes there," he went on. "You'll spend lots of weekends and other times with me. I'll be calling you every day and you can call me anytime you want to."

The children looked at each other, Luke looking especially lost. "Why do you have to do that?" he asked.

Linda explained, "Luke, you know Daddy and I argue a lot. We make each other angry and unhappy. I've thought a lot about it and feel it will be better and more peaceful for all of us if we live apart."

"You two are supposed to be our parents and you're

doing this? You're acting like teen-agers," Molly said angrily.

"Please, Molly," said David. He kissed both of them. Luke began to cry. "I don't want you to go. I'll be good. I won't play my drums anymore," he promised.

David swung Luke onto his lap, keeping his voice soft and slow to hold back the tears. He said, "Luke, baby, it's not your fault at all. I love you. We love you. You can even keep your drum at my apartment."

"I know you fight about me," said Luke. "You think I'm spoiled," he told his father.

"About me too," added Molly. "Mom thinks I should go to the day school next year and you always say, 'Public school was good enough for me and it's good enough for them.' But I don't care where I go. I'll go anywhere."

"Children," interrupted Linda, "we've disagreed about many things, sometimes about you, it's true. That doesn't mean that it's your *fault*. We both love you and we always will love you."

"Sure," Luke said sarcastically, "you don't love each other anymore. Maybe soon, you won't love us," he tested.

"Luke," Linda almost shrieked, "that's not true at all. The feelings between a man and a woman are different. We will always love you."

Why Once Is Not Enough

Being open with your child, explaining the reasons for the separation and the fact that it is not his fault is an important start in helping him deal with it. But it will be necessary to reinforce these points innumerable times.

Even where you have been frank with your child, problems may arise which you must be on the alert for. Soon after his father left, Luke was having difficulty sleeping at night and often did not want to go to school. One morning, over breakfast, he blurted out to his mother and began crying, "Once I said I wished Daddy didn't live here. I think that's really why he moved."

Tell your children, and then tell them *again,* that they're *not* responsible. It can be hard to convince children that the breakup is not their fault, when, indeed, you did fight about them a great deal.

"Sometimes parents argue about the children instead of the things that are really on their minds," says one psychiatrist. "Just assure your children that you may have argued about them and many other things as well. But that was because you think differently and disagree in general."

During a separation, psychiatrists say, adults go through a "mourning" period. They grieve over the life they lost and, what they see as their failure. At this trying time being ready, day in and day out, to talk to children about the same upsetting feelings they are having can be too much of a strain.

"I just couldn't hack it," explained one mother. "Every time Jeff brought up his father, the separation, or the way things used to be when we were all living together, I either cried, I got nasty to him, or I said something in anger about my husband. I'm over that now, but Jeff needed to talk *then* and I wasn't the person to help him, so I found someone who was."

If that is your case, get a professional to help your child talk over his guilt, his fears, and his anxieties. "Don't feel you're a failure as a parent if you can't talk about what's happened," says one psychiatrist. "You're being a good parent by getting him the help he needs." In addition, a well-trained professional—a child psychiatrist, child psychologist, or a social worker with experience in working with children of divorce—is objective and far more experienced at this sort of thing than you would be. If you ignore your child's needs, he may develop learning problems in school and have long-lasting unresolved emotional problems. With the stakes that high, a preventive effort seems more than worthwhile. (For a detailed discussion of how and when to look for a professional, see Part Five.)

For all the difficulties and dangers which come with separation and divorce, especially in the early stages, parents should remember that the most trying period will pass and, with parents and children helping and supporting each other, it can be followed by happier, more satisfying times.

Chapter Sixteen

RECONCILIATIONS AND CHILDREN

Following a separation, many men and women feel unsure that they did the right thing. They may waver between getting together and staying apart. This indecision is quite typical, but is hard on the children and on their own chances of setting up a new life.

Eleanor's feelings are typical of the way many newly separated men and women feel. They've expressed their anger, voiced their grievances, and put distance between themselves and the person they see as the source of their problems. Life is more peaceful and predictable than it had been during all the bad times. It is often lonely too.

If We Could Only Work Things Out

Then something unexpected happens. They begin to remember the good times. They think of the good qualities of the person they wanted out of their lives. And they admit some of their own mistakes ("He may not have shared my cultural interests, but he was a good father and his sense of humor was wonderful" . . . or . . . "She was never affectionate or very romantic, but, after all, she was the one who suggested we see a sex therapist and I refused to go").

And, of course, parents think of the children. Since the separation they seem so sad. They're not the same children. It would really be better for them, wouldn't it, if we got together again. And it was easier to handle the children when there were two of us. If we could work things out.

Many parents think seriously about trying again to work out their differences, as Eleanor did.

Confusing for Everyone

"I truly do not know what to do. We're thinking about trying a reconciliation, but the psychiatrist told us it would be unwise to experiment, to try living together, and then disappoint the children. If we seem so confused, she says, they might think we could leave them next.

"For that reason I don't bring up love. I say, 'Daddy and I don't get along. We argue too much.' I don't want them to think, 'Mommy loves us, but maybe next week she won't love us and she might leave.'

"I know our indecision makes it very hard on the children. When I'm rational, I know how bad it could be for them, but the truth is, I want Paul back. I guess I'm willing to risk making a mistake.

"Now he's alone. His girlfriend left. He's always been used to everyone giving him support and doing things his way. I think that's part of the reason he wants to go back. But for the last year we were together, he was terrible to the kids, yelling, mean. I'm afraid that will happen again.

"Right now he's very lovey-dovey to me and to the children. But at the same time, he tries to blame me for the separation. He still doesn't take responsibility for what he did and that makes me angry. He tells them, 'Mommy took you two thousand miles away.' But I had to get away from that place and that woman! Besides, Chicago had always been my home until we moved to California two years ago. All my family and friends are here.

"My older daughter was closer to her father than the other one. Sometimes I know she misses him a lot, but she remembers some of the bad times too when all he did was yell at her. Instead of saying how much she misses her father, she'll tell me how much she misses her best friend in California.

"One of the hard parts is that because I moved away, I have the children seven days a week and have full responsibility for them except when Paul comes in for a visit or the one or two times a year when the girls fly out to stay with him.

"There are other things we've been doing too that I know are confusing to the kids. When their father does come in for a visit, it's not just a Sunday. It's for several days. I don't let him stay overnight here, but when he takes the children out, he always says, 'Why doesn't Mommy come along?' I know it's wrong, but sometimes I do. We even went away for a weekend all together and later I realized it must have been traumatic for the girls. They were upset for some time. Lara, the little one, had terrible nightmares.

"This period is the hardest, though—not knowing what

we're going to do. But reconciliation requires a lot of dedication and self-awareness. Even with therapy, my husband only goes so far. He really doesn't *want* to change. He uses therapy as a boost. He likes to hear, 'You have to like yourself. You're a good person.' After that, he stops going. I honestly don't think it's going to work out."

Two months later:
"Now I know we're not going to go back. He really doesn't want to. But the girls are having a rough time. My little one said the other day, 'I want you and Daddy to go back together. How can I make it happen? When I don't see Daddy, I think he's dead. When I don't see you, I think you're dead. I don't want to lose one for the other.'

"And the older girl takes out her pain on the younger one. The little one asks her, 'Robin, why can't you love me?'

"Now I think we should have joint custody. I'm willing to move back to California. Maybe I secretly hope we'll still get back together, I don't know. But, anyway, now Paul says he doesn't want joint custody either. He says he can't handle it on a regular basis. I tell him the girls need him, but I guess I shouldn't force him to do it by making him feel guilty. It probably wouldn't be good for the girls. I'm really confused."

After several months, Eleanor and Paul did get back together and have been living in Chicago for six months. The outlook is doubtful. Eleanor says, "I know things aren't that good. Paul enrages me at times. The same old problems are still there. If I get to a point where I feel stronger and am more secure in my new job, I might turn the tables and tell him I want out."

Lawyers usually see these couples at an even later point, psychologically speaking, than do counselors or therapists. New York matrimonial attorney Barry Berger feels, "By the time they get to a lawyer, there isn't much chance for a reconciliation. Many have lived under the most adverse conditions for long periods of time—heavy drinking, violence, one party staying out nights. Most of them stayed in the thing longer than they should have because there's a tremendous inertia built into the institution of marriage. By the time they do get out, there's not much left."

Psychiatrists say they have little faith in the likelihood of success for reconciliations. But men and women who are contemplating getting back together would do well to consult a good marital therapist first, says Dr. Derdeyn. "Look at the real reasons for the split," he advises. "It may not be the marriage itself that is the problem. Marriage can be the scapegoat for work, ego, sexual, or other problems."

What to Tell the Children

Some couples will attempt reconciliations in spite of the odds against success. There are important things to remember if you are considering a reconciliation. First, children will cling to fantasies of their parents getting back together, especially where one parent wants it and keeps the idea alive. Do not mention *any* possibility of a reconciliation to the children until you are sure you are going to try.

Second, "Tell the children the truth, not made-up ideas," advises child psychiatrist Dr. Alan Levy. If you're trying to work things out, tell children this. The younger the children are, the simpler your explanation must be, but it can always be truthful. "Daddy and I are going to try to live together again and see if we can get along better and not argue so much. But we're not sure how it will work out" is one straightforward explanation. The moral here is—don't be afraid of your feelings.

If the reconciliation attempt fails, you have at least prepared your children for that possibility. Again, tell them the truth—that you both have tried your best, but that now you know it will be for everyone's good if you and their father (or mother) end the marriage once and for all.

Don't treat it as a tragedy. It is a step ahead. You are now absolutely convinced that the marriage is unworkable, and now that you're no longer vacillating between "Should I or shouldn't I?", you can get on with establishing a permanent lifestyle for yourself and your children. Your children need a definite plan for where and with whom they will live, how often they will see their other parent, and day-to-day routines and relationships aimed at building a life with one parent at a time, and a single lifestyle for you. *Your* happiness will be good for them!

Chapter Seventeen

IF YOU HAVE TO GO TO COURT

"He was drunk again. He called me a bitch and twisted my ankle in front of the children and said he wasn't leaving the house. He said he would get custody of the children. I couldn't let that happen. I went to court."

Charlotte, forty

"All litigations evoke intense feelings of animosity, revenge, and retribution . . . But none of them . . . can equal the sheer, unadulterated venom of a matrimonial contest," states well-known matrimonial attorney and author Louis Nizer. Child psychiatrist and author Richard Gardner adds, ". . . of all the forms of marital litigation the most vicious and venomous by far is custody litigation."

Judges in courtrooms across the country will make the

final decisions in more than 50,000 child custody cases this year. There will be right and wrong, good and bad, and justice and injustice done in those courtrooms.

Donald and Stephen

In the waiting room of Penn Station, Donald and Stephen are saying goodbye to their mother. "I'll write. I'll call. And we'll visit each other a lot," she tells them, kissing each one on his cheeks, his eyes, his ears. By the time she boards the train, they are all crying.

Donald is finally seeing it happen. After living in a home with fighting parents for as many of his twelve years as he can remember, the divorce is a fact.

It had not been easy for Donald, though. His father, a TV commentator, had had two psychiatrists interview Donald. They asked him questions like, "Which one of your parents do you spend more time with?" Donald answered that he spent more time with his father. He didn't get the opportunity to explain that his dad knew the city much better than his French-born mother and that his father *preferred* ball games and movies to all other pastimes.

One of the doctors had asked Donald, "If your mother and father were animals, what kinds of animals would they be?"

"My mother would be a beaver and . . . my father would be a fox," the boy responded.

Both psychiatrists inquired whether Donald had ever seen his mother drunk or breaking things, to which he replied, "No, never."

Eventually, each psychiatrist asked the tough question,

"Which one of your parents would you rather live with?"
Donald was reluctant to answer.

His mother had always been strict but, he felt, loved him dearly. If it weren't for her, the boy probably never would do his homework. His father brought him lots of presents like two record albums and a new soccer ball just that week and taught him every fine point about baseball. After several moments, Donald answered, without enthusiasm, that because he was a boy and was getting older, perhaps he would be better off with his father.

Donald's eight-year-old brother, Stephen, when later asked the same question by the same psychiatrists, said he would live with his mother *or* his father, but that he definitely wanted to stay with his brother. "Donny and me are sticking together," he said.

A long trial followed. It began before Christmas and was still going on when the boys got out of school for spring vacation. They heard hushed talk of lawyers and detectives, names of friends who testified for Mommy and others for Daddy. A newspaper story which Donald saw on the breakfast table one morning called this case, involving his well-known father, a television commentator, an important one because it would test whether fathers have equal rights to their children. The same article also pointed out, however, that their mother didn't seem as knowledgeable about her rights and didn't seem to have the same quality of legal advice as their father. The writer suggested that she may not have had her own money. When Donald read further that their mother had been crying on several occasions in court, but that their father had been calm, he thought, "Figures. Dad always told Mom she was too emotional."

When, at last, the judge was ready with his decision, he

explained that he was "respecting" what he thought were the boys' wishes. Custody would go to their father.

"The boys' wishes," Donald thought to himself. What does he know about our wishes? I *hate* this whole thing.

Standing on the train platform, Donald counts seven minutes before his mother's train will leave. The small financial settlement, and no employment prospects in New York for a forty-year-old former model who doesn't speak perfect English, forced his mother to move to Chicago where she would have a job in her brother-in-law's business.

As the train begins to move and Donald and Stephen stand motionless, each with one arm raised in a wave, Donald thinks it shouldn't have happened this way.

When All Else Fails

"The middle-income person with a legitimate custody grievance may not have a chance," one attorney told me.

"It's strictly a game for the rich," says another attorney who has spent many $150-hours in court on custody cases which required one hundred hours to try and as much to prepare for. "We don't want to go into court on custody, but people insist. We make the money and the kids get put through the mill."

People who don't have that kind of money have to settle for what they can get. There are family courts for those who live close to big cities which provide fast hearings as well as the services of social workers and translators for those who need them. But family courts tend to have large caseloads and short staffs and while their personnel are dedicated, the result often is rushed, inadequate discussion of the issues.

"I have on many days heard more than a hundred and twenty-five cases—with an average of less than three minutes per case!" wrote Simeon Golar, recently retired judge of the Family Court in New York City. "Certainly a judge needs more time to decide whether to take away a mother's child, or to have a man arrested or imprisoned for nonsupport . . . certainly those who appear before the court and the entire public are entitled to better than this."

The cost as well as the emotional suffering that comes with a custody trial has led such experts as Chief Justice Warren E. Burger to call for alternatives to the present system. They feel that it is essential to explore whether it is feasible to deal with such an intimate and sensitive relationship outside the courts. Many parents are convinced that it is indeed feasible.

One man who won custody of his three children after a bitter four-month battle in court says, "I think it would have been better to have put the whole thing before an arbitration panel. Once we had lawyers, we became more polarized than ever, sharpened our daggers, and were willing to spend every last penny for revenge." If the case been put before the American Arbitration Association's Family Dispute Service (see Chapter Twenty-Three), which provides the services of skilled mediators, referees, and arbitrators, the cost would have run in the neighborhood of $100 plus an hourly fee for the nonprofessional running the hearing, bringing the total cost up to roughly a few hundred dollars in comparison to the $10,000 to $20,000 spent on many contested custody cases. (See section on *How Much Will a Custody Case Cost?* in this chapter.)

Going to court is never a painless experience. It is upsetting, exhausting, possibly humiliating. Yet, if your spouse is suing for custody or if you are convinced that the only way you can get fair treatment is to sue, then go to court you must. Finding a good lawyer should be your first step.

Finding the Right Lawyer

"Maggie had been a good friend of mine in college," explained Judith. "I had seen her husband, Ben, a few times over the years and had heard he was a good attorney. After I separated from my husband, I hired him."

Judith and Ben may have made a good client-lawyer match, but it is more likely that it was disastrous. In choosing someone to represent you in a court fight over the custody of your children (as well as the other crucial issues that go with it—child support, alimony, division of property), there are specific guidelines to follow which can help you avoid a great many mistakes.

Unless your income is at or near the poverty level and qualifies you for a Legal Aid lawyer, or unless your case is of such a unique or special nature as to interest the Civil Liberties Union, you should follow the conventional steps in hiring an attorney.

1. Ask your friends or someone you trust for the name of a reputable attorney if you do not know one yourself. He may specialize in corporate law, tax law, real estate, patents, or be in general practice. He can serve as your *consultant*. When you meet with this person, don't equivocate or apologize in any way for not using him to represent you. Be direct and say, "Look, everything is on the line and I need a good trial lawyer who specializes in matrimonial law. Can you help me find one?"

If possible, get the names of more than one such attorney. The American Academy of Matrimonial Lawyers, which is based in Chicago, includes among its members some very competent attorneys. Those who apply and are accepted are well screened. They have passed tough oral and written examinations. "But," in the words of Philip Solomon, the organization's former president, "they tend to be expensive." Keep in mind, too, that some highly gifted matrimonial attorneys do not belong.

2. Make an appointment with the lawyer who is your first choice.

3. Ask him about his prior experience with custody cases and trials. How many has he handled? What were some of the specific details about the cases? (Of course, you wouldn't ask for names.) How did they turn out? After a while, you should get a feeling of how knowledgeable the man or woman is.

4. If you don't like the first lawyer you meet with, set up an appointment with another. You will be most satisfied with someone with whom you feel a rapport throughout what will be a long, highly emotional ordeal. While you want a skillful lawyer, think twice about one who suggests unethical tactics, such as "Don't give them any more money. Let's starve them into submission," or, "Take the kid and get out of the state," or, "Do something to get him to hit you. Then call the police."

A good recommendation and pleasant rapport are not your only criteria.

5. Because any custody trial is difficult to win, only a lawyer who is willing to work very hard in preparing your case will do. He will need to be up on all the fine points of the law; research the background of your life, your marriage, your spouse's life; line up witnesses who can

strengthen your case; familiarize himself with all the important details about your former spouse, new lovers in both your lives, relatives, and your children. He must know how and when to bring in expert witnesses such as psychiatrists, teachers, or other professionals and how to prepare those witnesses. In short, you must try to choose a man or woman who will explore all legitimate leads and possibilities in preparing and handling your case.

Before you hire an attorney, you might ask those whom you are considering whether they are arguing any cases at the moment. If so, tell them you would like to observe a trial for a morning.*

6. Discuss all fees in detail. What are their hourly rates? Do they want a retainer before they begin work on your case? How many hours do they think they will spend in court? Out of court in preparation?

Getting Started

"Mom, telephone for you," eleven-year-old Tracy called to her mother from the upstairs hall. "I think it's your lawyer."

"I'll take it in the kitchen," replied Mrs. McDonnell.

"Hello."

"Mrs. McDonnell? . . . Bill Davis. It's all set. Your husband, his lawyer, you and I will meet in my office Friday afternoon at 5:30."

"Oh . . . so soon?"

"Well, it's just an exploratory meeting. We have to go over income, tax returns, expenses, and the big question,

---

*Most courtrooms are open to the public. Where they are not, it is often possible to obtain written permission from a judge to observe.

210

custody. When the custody issue is settled, everything else will fall into place. Do you think he'll really fight for it or is he bluffing?"

"I wish I knew. Since the house, the money, and the kids usually go together, it's hard to know what's really on his mind. In his case, I almost think it's the house he doesn't want to lose. To be truthful, I guess neither of us does. We spent seven years restoring it, you know."

"Well, we'll find out a lot more after we get together on Friday."

"What shall I bring with me?"

"A list of expenses for yourself and your daughter. Make it as itemized as possible—housing, food, clothing, school, lessons, camp, transportation, miscellaneous items. And bring any receipts you have to back it up. Come a half hour early and we'll talk."

Once you have engaged a lawyer, the next step, while it may seem like asking for trouble, is usually a preliminary four-way meeting with your attorney, your spouse's attorney, and the two of you. The purpose of this usually uncomfortable procedure is to try to bring into the open more about what each party really wants and is willing to give up. Very often custody and visitation conflicts are smokescreens for the old frictions and anger that led to the divorce. "Until you sit down and start talking things out," Philip Solomon says, "you just don't know which demands are real and whether things are settleable or not. Sometimes they're not. Then the battle is on."

During these preliminary talks, it is common for parents to change their demands repeatedly, retract offers, or threaten to go to court over custody, visitation, child support, or alimony in hopes of getting a better deal. "All the while parents are trading their sons and daughters back and forth along with the station wagon, the jewelry, and the dining room set, they hope that these same children will remain happy, secure, and on the honor roll" is the way one veteran trial lawyer put it.

"Do you advise your female clients to ask for more money at these preliminary hearings than they expect to get or your male clients to offer less than they expect to pay?" I asked a well-known matrimonial attorney about a practice I had heard was common.

"I've tried it every way. I've tried being straight, exactly on the nose and we always end up haggling anyway and getting a bad deal," he told me.

"How much more does a woman generally ask for?" I inquired.

"Sometimes 30 to 40 percent more than she expects to get. Sometimes a little less."

Asking for more and offering less seems to be standard policy recommended by almost all the attorneys I spoke with.

"Of course," said one, "you have to negotiate."

Conciliation

Before you actually begin your custody trial, or following a preliminary hearing with a judge, you may be referred to a conciliation court or some other type of family counseling service connected to the court in certain states. These services make up a growing nationwide effort to help couples blunt some of the hostility which the adversary system normally encourages and resolve their differences over custody without going into court.

The Edwards—Gerard, Emily, and their children, Barbara, ten, and Thomas, seven (names and places have been changed)—arranged themselves in the semicircle of metal folding chairs in Room 3 at the Sierra Valley County Conciliation Court and waited. Judge Short, who presided at the preliminary hearing following Gerard's and Emily's separation, had strongly urged them to meet with a counselor in hopes of averting what promised to be a long custody battle.

Fred Hayes soon entered the plainly appointed room and after introducing himself as their counselor, he explained that one or two other staff members, a psychiatrist and a social worker, would also be participating in their talks. Then he asked Barbara and Thomas to wait in the playroom down the hall until he called them.

"What we try to do here is to think of the kids first," Fred told Gerard and Emily. "What do they need? What's going to be best for them? After all, they've already suffered. I know you don't want to make it any worse for them. And so began the first of four two-hour-plus sessions—at times loud, tearful, often painfully honest—with the counselors always nudging here, pulling there, steering the conversation back to what was best for the children.

One week later, after four sessions, the Edwards had had their eyes opened to some truths which their anger had been blinding them to. First, though they had stopped being husband and wife, they would always be father and mother to two children who totally depended on them. They realized that in their anger they had put their own need for revenge ahead of the children's needs. They also recognized that their continued fighting upset the children and stood in the way of their development.

Gerard and Emily agreed that the children would live

with Emily, but that Gerard would see them for at least one day each weekend, one weekday evening and over-night, one month in the summer, on alternate birthdays, on Thanksgiving or Christmas each year and for any other reasonable request. They made an appointment to come back six weeks later to discuss how their agreement was working.

"This type of conciliation service must save families a great deal of anguish and it probably saves the taxpayer money in courtroom time and staff expenses," I said to Brinkley Long, the Director of Family Court Services for Sacramento County in California, after learning that approximately fifty percent of all cases referred to concil-iation courts are settled without a court battle. "Why aren't there more of these conciliation courts?" I asked.

"Well, it takes a certain amount of money—not a great deal, our staff is small . . . six counselors, three typists, and some are part-time—to set up a conciliation court. Elected officials are often reluctant to ask for tax-levy funds for new projects. So, even though we're cost effective, funding is a problem."

At the time of this writing, only sixteen counties in California have conciliation courts. Counties in some other states provide some degree of family counseling to accomplish similar objectives but not in as systematic a program as these parts of California offer. Proposition Thirteen may lead to cutbacks or stand in the way of expansion of the California program.

Most families on a collision course over custody will not have the benefit of effective counseling. Others will reject the conciliator's recommendations, sometimes insisting on a full-blown trial because of a conscious or uncon-

214

scious wish to punish the other parent. Each of these groups will end up in court.

How to Protect Yourself. What to Guard Against

If you are thinking about separating or already have, and you and your lawyer are preparing your case, you will not want to do anything to jeopardize your standing in court. Both men and women should guard against making some all-too-common mistakes.

"The worst label for a man is 'a man of violence,' " says one matrimonial attorney who cautions men to "avoid all threats and physical violence. After a while a woman starts writing down threats or physical abuses. When she's up on that witness stand, and recites from her notes, 'On January fifth, he said, "I'll kill you"; on February twenty-seventh, "I'll break your legs." On March twenty-third, "I'll smash your face," ' the judge is not going to look kindly on him.

"Sometimes what a woman says is not all true, or the woman may have provoked the guy. She knows his boiling point and the right trigger words. Usually something about his sexual performance or his job. But even if the judge accepts 50 percent of what she said, he's in trouble."

"A woman should avoid screaming fights," says another lawyer. "Neighbors can be brought in to testify and she'll look unstable."

Calling names in front of children can be evidence against you in the courtroom as can drinking, or drug problems, or rarely spending time with one's children. If witnesses come in and say, "I never see Mrs. B. with her children. They're usually with their father or a baby-sitter," it looks bad for the mother.

Above all, violence, emotional instability, verbal abusiveness, heavy drinking, not giving time or showing concern for one's children will seriously damage a parent's chances in court.

How to Help Your Lawyer

The man or woman you retain to represent you may be an outstanding trial attorney who knows how to prepare, question, and cross-examine witnesses. Yet, he needs your help. You must give him as much information as you can about income and assets of yourself and your spouse. (Whether you end up in court or not, you want to get the most favorable financial settlement possible.) For a discussion of custody and money, see Chapter Seventeen. Give him a lot of possible witnesses, people who are familiar enough with and willing to testify about your character behavior and that of your spouse, your children's emotional adjustment, their behavior and performance at school.

Insist that your lawyer prepare you as fully as possible for anything the opposition might ask you on the witness stand. "Duplicate courtroom conditions," advises one attorney who familiarizes his witnesses with the typical questions and strategies they can expect.

How Long Will a Custody Trial Take?

In order for the case for each side to be fully developed, the parties and their witnesses are questioned and cross-examined at length. Important witnesses may spend hours on the stand. They are often recalled at one or more points in a case.

Experienced attorneys put the average number of *courtroom* hours in a custody case at between fifty and seventy-five. An equal number of hours are usually spent preparing the case outside of court and courtroom days are virtually never consecutive.

"Court calendars are crowded and cases usually take longer than expected. So judges have to break them up and fit them in wherever they have time," explains a busy Chicago lawyer. "A case that takes eighty hours in court may be spread over a period of two to four months. Then the judge can take another two weeks to write his decision."

Other delays result in cases where damaging evidence comes up and an attorney asks for a delay in order to prepare an argument against the new evidence. There can be further delays while the judge waits for reports from psychiatrists or social workers and then for the time necessary to study them himself.

Once in court, you are dependent on the intelligence, openmindedness, biases, and conscientiousness of the man or woman in black robes looking down at you from the massive, raised bench. Most judges are at their very best in custody trials. They painstakingly search for the truth and for the child's best interests. Some do brilliant work and their decisions have influenced the way child custody is generally handled. But the system has its flaws. Even the most conscientious judge cannot always know how much weight to give such evidence as a father's "cured" alcoholism, a mother's occasional use of cocaine, a father's brief homosexual liaison several years prior to his marriage, the fact that a mother had wanted to abort the child she now wants custody of, or a father's numerous periods of unemployment.

While many judges are highly competent and willing to call in experts to help in explaining complex human issues as well as technical psychiatric points, parents can't always count on justice being done. Occasionally one hears hair-raising accounts of the courtroom travesties which make the placing of a custody decision in unknown hands such a major risk. Michael's is a case of bad risk.

"I could hear the judge clearly. He was discussing a touch football game with his law clerk that was coming up that Sunday. They talked during the time I was giving some of my most important testimony," he explained about a Nassau County, New York judge. "And he didn't pay attention at many other points in the case. And, at the end of the case, with twenty-nine hundred pages of testimony, he gave his decision in one hour. He didn't even *look* at the testimony! Some of it was from months before, so he couldn't have remembered it all. Some time later, I discovered that the judge retired two days after he gave his decision. No wonder he didn't want to bother going over testimony or taking time to write his decision.

"Now my lawyer's preparing our appeal. But that's an uphill battle," said a discouraged Michael. (See the next chapter for a discussion of appealing a custody arrangement or decision.)

Being on the Witness Stand

In a custody battle in court, you will have to answer questions under oath put to you by your own and your spouse's lawyer. Your attorney will prepare questions designed to bring out your strengths as a parent while the opposition, during your cross-examination, will try to reveal and reiterate any weaknesses he can find. At a later point, your own attorney can call you back to the stand for what is called redirect examination, in which he can straighten out any misconceptions which may have come up during the cross-examination, but he may not bring up any new points. Then, the other attorney can do a recross if he wishes, but again the focus narrows and he can cover only what came up in the redirect questioning.

Testifying on the witness stand is a high-pressure experience where it helps to be as well-prepared as possible and appear sure of yourself. And even then, you can't be prepared for everything.

"Mrs. Lawson, please tell the court your full name."
"Mary Louise Sherwood Lawson."
"And, Mrs. Lawson, where do you live?"
"On West Edgewood Drive in Greenmont."
"How old are you?"
"Thirty-nine."
"Please tell us the names and ages of your children."
"Edward is eleven. Nicholas is nine and Jessica is four."
"What is your educational background, Mrs. Lawson?"
"I have a B.A. degree in history and I completed an M.A. in education two years ago at the state university."
"Are you employed?"
"No."
"Have you been offered employment and, if so, at what salary?"
"Yes, I have been offered two jobs, one as a fifth-grade teacher at the Lake Drive School in Greenmont at a salary of $14,000 per year, the other as a remedial reading teacher in North Haven at a salary of $13,500 a year."

"Did you accept either job offer?"

"No, I did not. I've decided to stay at home full-time until my daughter starts the first grade. In the meantime, I am taking further courses and am working toward earning a professional certificate in teaching children with learning disabilities."

"Mrs. Lawson, why are you seeking custody of your three children?"

"Because I love them and I'm convinced that they're better off with me than with anyone else."

"Were you surprised to learn that your husband wanted custody of the children?"

"Yes, I was. Ever since Eddie was born, it's been difficult to get John to spend time with them. Whenever any of my courses were in the evening, he wanted to know my schedule. He said that he would plan to be out on those nights and I should have a baby-sitter come because he didn't want to get involved with baths or dinner or homework."

"I have no further questions, Your Honor."

Husband's attorney: "Your Honor, may we approach the bench?"

Judge: "Yes. Both counsels come forward."

(Five minutes later) Judge: "I'm going to ask the bailiff to have the two Lawson children who are present removed for a short time. Bailiff? . . . Thank you . . . Proceed."

Husband's attorney (cross-examining wife): "Mrs. Lawson, was your marriage to Mr. Lawson your first marriage?"

"No."

"Tell us about your previous marriage or marriages, please."

"I was married once before when I was eighteen years old and divorced when I was nineteen."

"Was there a child from that marriage?"

"Yes."

"Where is that child today?"

"My husband had disappeared and I . . . I gave the child up for adoption."

"I have no further questions, Your Honor."

Judge: "You may step down, Mrs. Lawson."

Children on the Witness Stand

Most judges in custody cases want to know first-hand what children think and feel about each of their parents. Psychiatrists' direct testimony and written reports, private talks in chambers between judge and child, without parents or attorneys present, and direct testimony in open court by children give judges a chance to learn this information.

Judges usually view children's testimony differently from the testimony of adults, however. The first concern is how valid and fully thought through they feel a child's testimony is. Is he mature enough to think clearly or is he responding to feelings of the moment? (Did Mommy scold him this morning for not putting his clothes away? or did Daddy refuse to buy him a new baseball glove? and, therefore he is favoring the other parent?)

And then they are concerned about whether a child has been influenced, pressured, threatened, or just cajoled into a certain point of view. New York psychiatrist Dr. Marie Friedman, who has performed numerous custody evaluations, feels, "A child is always influenced. The question is how much?"

If your child is scheduled to testify or to be interviewed in chambers by a judge, you may worry that his other parent has tried to "brainwash" him into thinking that he or she should be his choice as custodial parent. You may also feel that you should try your best to sell yourself to your child before the crucial meeting of judge and child.

A good judge should be able to cut through the propaganda. "I always ask a child indirectly whether his parents talked to him about coming to see me," said one judge. "After talking with a child for a couple of hours, I can usually find out what his true feelings are."

Many parents and judges feel children should not testify in open court or at all, or at least not if they are under approximately thirteen years of age. The children would face cross-examination which, while never harsh toward a young witness, is upsetting because of the highly personal subject matter. Where a child is a preteenager, the judge usually does not have the child appear in court but meets with him in his chambers and hopes that he will be able to uncover the truth. "The most important thing is getting kids to trust you when you say that everything that goes on between you is confidential, that their parents will not know anything of what was said," explained Judge Kassal.

Judges and psychiatrists say they are concerned about children feeling guilty or having loyalty conflicts later on because they favored one parent over the other. Psychiatrists say that children often cannot foresee or express the fact that they might regret their stand later on. It is only parents who can protect their children from what can be devastating guilt. Children should be allowed to express

222

their opinions without being made to feel guilty about them or that they are responsible for whatever problems their other parent has because they made their parent unhappy. Parents shouldn't see it as a popularity contest but as what environment is better for the child's development.

What Is a Psychiatric Evaluation?

In the imperfect forum of a courtroom where human behavior must be analyzed, characters judged, and relationships evaluated, judges frequently call upon "behavioral scientists," usually psychiatrists or psychologists, for technical assistance in gathering as much meaningful information as possible.

These psychiatric evaluations usually begin with the judge appointing a psychiatrist or psychologist to examine all the important individuals in the children's home lives. This includes the children themselves, both parents, new live-in partners or spouses if there are any, and possibly, close relatives or housekeepers.

Such a court-appointed expert will interview each party individually for a period of hours. An interview with a parent will cover his or her childhood, schooling, early friendships, relationships with parents, military service record, job history, relationships with and feelings toward his children, and any new love attachments. It will try to get at the parent's character and his or her real attitude toward the children.

When interviewing children, the psychiatrist or psychologist looks at the general psychological condition of the child. Is he functioning in school? Does he have friends? Does he have a good opinion of himself? What does he say about his mother and father—the good and the bad parts?

One or both attorneys may have a separate psychiatric evaluation performed for various possible reasons: They may wish to be doubly certain of a fair hearing; they may be concerned that the court-appointed person has interpreted some information unfavorably, they might believe that the court's expert is not competent or thorough enough to get all the vital information, or, they simply may want to try to get an advocate—someone on their side. Many professionals will not cooperate in this kind of examination, however.

"Some parents call me and say, 'Doctor, I want you to interview me and my child and write a report on whether you think I am a good parent,' " says child psychiatrist Dr. Frank Curran. "I tell them that my procedure in custody evaluations includes the interviewing of all parties several times, often using diagnostic tests. I tell them that I can't guarantee my recommendation. When they hear that, they usually don't use me.

"The reason I like to see both parents as well as the child interacting with each parent is that otherwise I find I often get an unbalanced picture. And some children are overly influenced by one parent," Dr. Curran explained. "Before I had this policy, I once had a twelve-year-old boy in here. When I asked him to tell me about his father, he said:

'He doesn't care about me.'

'Why doesn't he care about you? I asked him,' Dr. Curran went on.

'Because he won't buy me the new skateboard I want.'

'How much does it cost?'

224

'Fifty dollars,' the boy told me.
'Do you have a skateboard?'
'Yeah.'
'How much was that one?'
'Twenty-five dollars'."

There are professionals who will evaluate just one parent, with or without children, testify in court, and write an opinion for the judge as to whether this person is a fit parent or is capable of being one. While such reports may represent the honest opinion of the expert, they usually have less impact on the judge's thinking than that of a more thorough evaluation done on all of the parties by an impartial, court-appointed psychiatrist. There are exceptions, of course. If an attorney were able to prove serious flaws and inconsistencies in the testimony of a court-appointed expert, for instance, his evaluation would then be regarded in a dubious light.

In the words of one attorney who has discredited some expert witnesses on the stand, "It has happened that a psychiatrist has been destroyed." He explains, "Some experts have prejudices that I get at in roundabout ways—prejudices usually favoring mothers having custody of their children, for example. I may reveal some inconsistencies to them which they overlooked in their reports and then they start equivocating, saying that this new information might be reason to modify their recommendation, that they can't be sure, and so on. Once they start wavering, I've got them."

Psychiatrists and psychologists are part of most custody cases for good reason, however. Lawyers and judges are in agreement that the behavioral scientists add important expertise and insight and that the process of reaching custody decisions is greatly improved by their participation.

What About Private Investigators?

Private investigators are usually not needed or appropriate in custody cases and can even damage a parent's chances at winning. "Don't let a detective practice law for you," warns attorney Berger. "It can be a big mistake to go to a private investigator without getting good legal advice first. Surveillance itself can be considered a form of cruelty," he explains. "Always consult your lawyer on anything having to do with your case." Occasionally, though, private investigators are used.

Adultery is rarely grounds for divorce today. Many states allow no-fault divorce and some others accept lesser grounds such as "irreconcilable differences." In those states where adultery is one of the few acceptable grounds for immediate divorce, many people avoid having to use it or similarly distasteful charges by waiting out the required legal separation period (usually one year) and then applying for what amounts to a no-fault divorce.

However, the issue of adultery often surfaces in custody cases as part of an attempt by one parent to discredit the character of the other. Although few judges would consider an implication of adultery or even a discreet adulterous act proof of a parent's unfitness, by today's standard of "the better parent," any such evidence can be damaging to a parent's "moral fitness" quotient in a closely contested custody battle. Detectives are often used to track down the kind of information in Mrs. Falk's case:

Husband's attorney: "Mrs. Falk, when were you and your husband legally separated?"

"On December sixteenth, just about six weeks ago."

"Mrs. Falk, did you enter an apartment building at 111

Michigan Avenue at approximately ten-thirty P.M. on the night of Tuesday, October third?"

"I think I might have."

"Were you in the company of a man by the name of Herbert Griffin?"

"Yes."

"At what time did you leave Mr. Griffin's apartment?"

"I don't remember. An hour or so later, I think."

"Wasn't it actually two A.M. when you and Mr. Griffin left his building, after which he escorted you home in a taxi?"

"I don't remember exactly."

"Is this photograph of a man with his arm around a woman a picture of you and Mr. Griffin entering his apartment building?"

"Yes, it seems to be."

"What relation is Mr. Griffin to you?"

"A friend."

"I have no further questions."

Andrea Caldwell, thirty-four, was separated, hadn't worked since she was twenty-one, and lived upstairs in a two-family house in Brooklyn, New York, which her parents owned and where they occupied the downstairs apartment. Andrea was concerned about her husband Sam's threat to fight for custody of their two children and his statement that "I'm going to see what I can get on you." Because they were not yet legally separated, Andrea knew it would help her chances in court if a private investigator could help her to get something on Sam, such as proving that he was intimate with other women. She decided to talk to a detective.

After making an appointment with someone at a detective agency in a building where a friend worked,

Andrea was due to meet with a Mr. Logan of the Star Detective Bureau, Inc., at ten o'clock on a Tuesday morning.

"My husband and I are not living together anymore," she began in Mr. Logan's office. "He took a studio apartment outside of town, but we haven't signed separation papers. He says he wants custody of the children and I think he may be having me followed."

"What makes you think that, Mrs. Caldwell?" Mr. Logan asked.

"He said he was going to get something on me."

"Is there anything he can get on you? Have you been going out with other men?"

"Well, I have gone out a few times, but I've never stayed out for the night or had a man stay overnight in my apartment."

"You know, Mrs. Caldwell," he explained, "the courts go by a decision which was written some years ago. It has to do with what they call 'opportunity and inclination.' This means that if you're in a man's apartment or he is in yours for two or three hours and there has been any sign of affection between you—any sign—a kiss, holding hands, an arm around the other person, it is presumed that adultery has taken place."

"So he may have evidence against me already?" Andrea asked.

"It's possible, though we don't even know for sure that anyone has followed you," he answered.

Andrea finally got to the main point. "Mr. Logan, if there's any chance that he has something on me, I'll be at a great disadvantage. At least I'd like to try to get the same thing on him. How can you help me?"

"Do you know for a fact that your husband is going out with any women?"

"No, I don't know what he is doing. All I know is that I might need all the help I can get if we ever go to court."

"Well, it's an expensive proposition. We don't know how many days it might take—if we turn up anything at all. But, let me tell you how we work," Mr. Logan went on.

"For one thing, we charge twenty dollars an hour and our minimum is eight hours. For two men, it would be thirty dollars an hour, but I think one man would do. The charge for a car is twenty-five dollars a day. That comes to a hundred eighty-five dollars a day plus expenses, per eight-hour tour for one man. Should you decide to go ahead, I would suggest we start on a Thursday or Friday evening and hope we turn up something quickly."

"What do I get after you're through?" Andrea inquired.

"You get a written report and any photographs we can get. We only photograph in the street or in public places—no breaking down doors," Mr. Logan said. "And we have to have good pictures of your husband to make a positive i.d. as well as his exact home and office address."

"At a hundred eighty-five dollars a day, I might be able to afford you for a day or two. I'll have to think about it. Thank you, Mr. Logan," Andrea said.

While Andrea Caldwell may have thought she was simply protecting herself, she could have damaged her case in the long run.

There certainly are custody cases where good detective work can make an important difference—in establishing the hours a parent keeps, the company he travels with, activities he engages in, his style of living, and the amount of time he is with his children—but it can be a double-edged weapon and should be used only with the advice of a lawyer.

How Much Will a Custody Case Cost?

An average custody case would run for approximately fifty to seventy-five courtroom hours, roughly seven to nine days. It would require a minimum of thirty hours—probably more—for preliminary talks, research, and preparation of witnesses by an attorney. If a lawyer charges $100 per hour, which is less than most top matrimonial attorneys in large cities charge, the basic bill would be about $8,000.

A more protracted case, requiring a total of 200 hours for preparation and trial work, at the not unusual charge of $125 per hour, would cost $25,000 in straight legal fees. In addition, some well-known lawyers demand a bonus of several thousand dollars over and above their fee if they win the case for their client.

Unfortunately, the parent with less money may lose the custody case although he (or more usually, she) may be the better parent. Top lawyers, psychiatrists, psychologists, and private investigators can make the difference in the outcome of a close case. These experts may be beyond the financial means of one party but not the other. A woman who does not have direct access to money to pay the attorney's fees may find that she cannot get any lawyer at all, least of all one who is tops in the field. Lawyers are becoming more and more reluctant to take cases where they do not get paid until the case is settled. They no longer want to rely on the hope that the judge will assign the husband to pay his wife's lawyer in full. "Often, the husband never pays or takes years to pay," says attorney Berger.

The truth is that certain custody cases can be presented properly and thoroughly only with extensive research, expert advice, many expensive hours of testimony and cross-examination of witnesses and, above all, a large expenditure of money.

The high cost of getting an adequate hearing on a custody issue creates a most unfair situation for many women and men—the woman who doesn't have access to enough money to engage as able a lawyer as her husband; or the middle-income man who may want custody and has a legitimate claim but does not have the money to go to court for an extended period of time, and simply gives in to the still prevalent prejudice favoring mothers having custody.

Lawyers for Children

"Children should become more consumeristic," says one prominent Denver child psychiatrist. "Their interests need to be represented by having their own attorney."

The law allows judges who feel it appropriate to appoint a lawyer for a child in the person of a law guardian, who is paid relatively modestly by the court or is with a nonprofit organization such as the Civil Liberties Union. His or her status in the courtroom is less than that of the parents' attorneys.

A law guardian, or guardian *ad litem*, is permitted to participate in the custody hearing, to subpoena and question witnesses, cross-examine the parties or witnesses testifying for either party, and make a recommendation concerning the child's custody decision. But the child is not a *party* to the action as are his parents. This means that while the parents, through their attorneys, may appeal the final decision, the child may not.

In spite of the limitations, many children have been helped because judges appointed law guardians for them. Parents' interests are not always the same as children's and while they often overlap, they may conflict at times. For instance, where children favor the less likely parent— where they want to be with their father rather than their mother, or their stepmother instead of their natural father; or where a judge is not skilled enough at interviewing children to get at their true feelings—an advocate specifically for the child makes it more likely that the child's interests will be represented. For this reason, many feel that this policy should lead to full representation for every child in every custody case. Others argue the dangers of adding more fuel to the already fiery adversary climate. Still others are put off by the additional cost in an already overburdened legal system, which would have to be assumed by the taxpayer or the parents.

The most convincing reason for children having full representation in custody decisions (in or out of court), as a legal right, seems to be that it would guarantee scrutiny of *every* custody agreement, not only disputed ones. Just because his parents have agreed on a custody plan does not guarantee that it is the best possible arrangement for the child.

If a child had his own counsel, he would also be protected against the many postponements that are almost routinely asked for by one or both parents or their attorneys. They tend to ignore the child's need for a quick decision so that he can get back to a permanent and predictable living arrangement. As we have said, prolonged interruptions in his life can be genuinely damaging. Because a child's emotional attachments are still vulnerable to time and other influences, continuity in his relationships and fast settlements in custody matters are crucial to a child's well-being.

Chapter Eighteen

CAN CUSTODY BE CHANGED?

On the last day of school before the start of Christmas vacation, nine-year-old Jennifer said to her teacher, "Mrs. Hart, I don't know if I'll be back here after vacation. My mother and father are divorced and now they're fighting about where I should live. My father says I'm going to go and live with him. I hope I don't have to move though. You're the best teacher I ever had."

Many custody arrangements agreed to by parents are reversed at a later time—months or even years later—when one parent relocates, remarries, otherwise changes his circumstances, or simply changes his mind. Or when a child asks for a change. Custody issues decided by judges can be appealed immediately following the decision or reopened months or years later. In fact, many decisions involving the custody of children are virtually never final.

A Serious Step

Mothers and fathers as well as experts caution parents to consider the implications carefully before they try or agree to change their child's custody arrangement. Uprooting a child and moving him to a new home with a new person in charge can have far-reaching effects. Many such changes have turned out to be disruptive and ill-advised.

Henry, in his intention to do what was best for his children, underestimated his own ability as a parent, his children's love for him, and their need for continuity. At the same time, he placed too much value on what he thought was the children's primary need—to live with their mother.

Some time after the divorce, Henry's former wife, Edna, became ill and was hospitalized with a long-term chronic illness. Henry took their two boys and one girl to live with him where they struggled with single-parent family life for four years. In spite of the mixups in laundry, the "everybody pitches in" casualness, and a house that fell somewhere between being spotless and chaotic, the children seemed happy, did well in school, had friends, and took on responsibilities.

Rightly believing it was correct as well as healthy for the children, Henry encouraged them to talk about their mother, to love her, to write letters to her, and to send her small gifts on holidays.

When Edna was released from the hospital in what doctors said was a remission period which could last for years, she demanded that the children return to live with her. Henry believed that the children might benefit from being with their mother after such a long separation. Because custody had never officially been given to him, he simply and voluntarily told the children that they would be moving back to their mother's house. They protested but Henry appeased them by promising that he would see them at least twice a week or more if they wished.

No one could have been more surprised than Henry when he took a call from Edna in his office one morning in early September saying she and the children were at the airport. "I've decided to move down to Palm Beach where Mother and Dad are. They've taken an apartment for us and we'll live on my trust money. I'm doing it now before the new school year starts. It's just too boring in the suburbs up here," she said. "The children are upset, but they'll get over it. Goodbye Henry." Henry was tied down to his job in Chicago for at least another seven years when he could begin collecting a pension for twenty-five years of service. He was heartbroken at not seeing his children regularly but couldn't afford to leave, whereas Edna's parents were wealthy and had told her that she and the children could live anywhere she chose. Nor did it occur to Henry that he could fight for custody, that he might have won, and that he might be a better parent than Edna.

So for the next several years, until his children became of college age and were more mobile, Henry only visited them for a week during each Christmas season and for two weeks every summer. It was some compensation to Henry to learn that all his hard, loving work as a parent had not been wasted. During one of his visits, his daughter, then twelve, slipped a note into his pocket at

237

the airport just as he was to board. When he was alone on the plane a short time later, Henry read the note. It said, "Dear Daddy, I'll *always* love you. Love, Kimmy."

Procedures for Changing Custody

It is rare for a parent to volunteer to change custody as Henry did. Much more often it is done under pressure or through the courts. When and if you consider trying to force a custody change, keep in mind that judges and psychiatrists give priority to maintaining a child's continuity. A child's emotional attachments are more tenuous and vulnerable than an adult's. He needs as much external stability from his parents and his environment as possible, especially where there has been a divorce and a child has already had more than his share of upsets.

If, after considering this, you still feel your child would be better off with you than with your former spouse and you see no other choice, you can fight for legal custody through the courts in one of two ways. (Changing custody without legal sanction, child-snatching, is discussed in Chapter Twenty, Custody Disasters.)

If you did not have a legal battle over custody but had a private agreement until the time you decided that there should be a custody change, you can take your case to court.* You will need the services of a competent trial lawyer, experienced in custody matters (see preceding chapter). You will have to present strong justification and evidence in order to expect a judge to disrupt your child's

---

*If you had specified in your original separation agreement that any future custody dispute would go before arbitration, you can then enlist the services of the nationwide American Arbitration Association. Or, you can apply for it now. (See Chapter Twenty-Two.)

living arrangements and run the risk of having the court become a revolving door for custody disputes.

But suppose you have already been to trial over the custody issue and some weeks after the close of courtroom proceedings you are informed by mail that the judge has ruled in favor of the opposing side. You disagree with the ruling and feel strongly that the evidence presented in the case was really in your favor. You must act quickly. Within thirty days (check with your lawyer as to the exact time period in your state) of receiving written notice of the judge's decision, your lawyer must file a notice of appeal with the next higher court. While getting to the appeal may require several months, it is a law that the notice of appeal must be made within that first month in many states and within a similarly limited period in all states.

Once you have filed the notice of appeal there is an interim measure open to you. If you feel that the judge overlooked a point of law or a favorable piece of evidence, you can ask to have your case *reargued* in front of the same judge. If your reargument efforts are successful, you can cancel the notice of appeal.

An appeal can be based *only* on the facts on the court record. *No* new evidence is permitted. This is an important reason for making certain that your attorney introduces all information at your custody trial which might be helpful to your case, including: your child's relationship with you; his adjustment; his schoolwork; the stability of the home you plan to provide; as well as any features about your former spouse's ability as a parent—time he or she gives to the child, or anything about his or her character, stability, and friends—which might be in your favor.

The appeal is heard by a court higher than the trial

court. Judges are unlikely to overturn considered decisions of lower courts without compelling reasons. In order to stand a chance of a higher court overturning a trial court's decision, lawyers and judges say that the record of your trial must show that the trial court committed such error or abused its discretion to a point that was clearly damaging to your child. Instances where an appeal might be successful and a ruling changed would include: Those where the judge ignored the wishes of an older child; where he never interviewed a child; or where he completely ignored the testimony and recommendations of a psychiatrist or family counselor. It is possible that a judge in such a case would be willing to hear a reargument. Often judges refuse, however, and the next step is an appeal. Before an Appellate Court (or the equivalent of the next higher court) will consider your case, they may call in both lawyers in the case in an effort to settle it, or at least to limit the issues and narrow the focus, thereby cutting down on the volume of paper submitted by lawyers and the time required of judges.

Where a case cannot be settled, you will get the appeal you asked for. But bear in mind that most appeals are denied. Should you lose your appeal, you may or may not be able to go higher—for example, in New York, to the State Court of Appeals. That highest state court will not hear a second appeal if the lower court, the Appellate Division, was unanimous in voting against you. On the other hand, if the Appellate Division made modifications in the trial court's decision or if the judges split their decision, the Court of Appeals may feel your case warrants another hearing.

The other way of using the courts in attempting to change your custody arrangement would be by reopening an old case based on a *new* set of facts; this new set of facts is usually referred to as a "material change in circumstances." Some parents mistakenly believe that a change in *financial* circumstances or in lifestyle constitutes "material change" and could convince a judge to move a child, but it is the quality of life a judge attempts to evaluate.

"I care about the psychological welfare of a child," explained one judge. "I look at who gives him love, time, discipline, not who can provide him with a bigger room or fancier gadgets to play with."

In order to uproot a child from the parent, home, school, friends, and neighborhood to which he is attached, it must be proven that his parent is no longer caring for or protecting him in a manner that will allow him to grow and develop in as healthy a fashion as his other parent could.

In one such case, Carl brought suit against his wife, Martha, who had won custody of their eight-year-old son, Erik, two years earlier at the time Carl and Martha were divorced.

During a weekend visit with Carl and his new live-in girlfriend, Erik reported that his mother's boyfriend, Peter, had given him "this white stuff to sniff. It was called coke, Daddy. Is that like Coca-Cola?" the boy asked.

During the trial which followed, it came out that (1) Peter had let Erik sniff cocaine (through dollar bills) on at least five occasions with the boy's mother present; (2) Erik kept late hours, on school nights, often staying downstairs until midnight in the bar and restaurant which Peter ran; and (3) Martha and Peter's bedroom door did not close all the way and on several occasions, Erik had walked in on their lovemaking.

On the morning of what was to be the fourth day of testimony, Martha came to the judge's chambers fifteen minutes before he was due in the courtroom. "I'm ready to call it quits, Judge," Martha said. "I think Erik would be better off with his father."

"It appears that way to me, too," said the judge. "But I hope you won't cut yourself off from Erik. You are his mother and he does need you—provided, of course, you act responsibly."

"I've learned a lot, Judge. I will see Erik. I just hope I haven't let too much damage take place."

I cannot stress enough how much judges discourage parents' use of the courts to accomplish anything other than furthering a child's best interests.

Knowing that many parents can get caught up in custody battles because of their own anger and may not realize at the time how disruptive the experience is to children's welfare, some experts, including Dr. Albert Solnit of the Yale Child Study Center, child psychiatrist Anna Freud, and Yale University law professor Joseph Goldstein, have gone so far as to advise that ". . . each child placement be final and unconditional . . . not subject to modification."

While this thinking is not, and probably will not become, law, there is a growing attitude among law-makers and judges that it should be extremely difficult to change custody.

There is no doubt that you should put your most considered effort into your first custody agreement (or trial) because it will probably be your best opportunity.

Chapter Nineteen

CUSTODY AND MONEY

Money—how much you have and how you use it—has a crucial effect on how you and your children adjust to the breakup of your marriage.

A word of caution first, though. Accountants, lawyers and parents who have lived through many a horror connected with money and divorce warn that the most devastating experiences in separations occur when money becomes a tool for avenging anger and punishing a spouse. Closing charge accounts, running up large bills, unilaterally emptying bank accounts, or taking out a second mortgage on a home and leaving the other spouse with the payments may provide a few sweet moments of revenge on a husband who ran off with a younger woman or a wife who left because she wanted "more out of life," but it creates a war-zone climate in which the children of the divorce are the most severely wounded.

"I dropped the children off at the bus stop and went to work one morning," one shocked man reported. "When I got home, all the furniture was gone. My ex-wife still had a key and she had hired a moving truck to take everything away."

It is usually and understandably difficult for a separated couple to come to agreements on money matters. However, children's best interests are served if money problems are handled straightforwardly. If both parents keep this in mind, they should find that it takes at least some of the bitterness out of their financial negotiations.

If You Have Custody—Mother

Money can be a lifeline. Children are an enormous economic strain. The cost of raising a child to the age of eighteen is estimated to be about $55,000. In the struggle to cope with your children's emotional and financial demands as well as with your own doubts about whether you're up to handling all the household, family, job, and social responsibilities of a single parent, financial peace of mind gives you something to hold on to.

Your concerns will be different from those of most men. For you, being sure of having enough money means:

1. knowing your rights in order to obtain the most advantageous financial settlement.

2. getting a job or making definite plans to train for the work you would like to do.

The fact is, financial independence has become a necessary objective for almost all women. The woman who elects to become a full-time homemaker and who has no personal financial resources or marketable skill is courting disaster. A full-time homemaker who is divorced after fifteen or twenty years of marriage usually loses husband, support, and status in one swoop. She has no job, no marketable education or job skills, no Social Security, no share in her husband's pension. She may have child-support payments but they are not likely to be generous and her alimony may also be less than generous and probably short-term.¹ On top of all this, she discovers that she no longer sees many of the friends from her married life.

While some of your problems will subside when you and your husband split up, one will not. Expenses.

"After my husband moved out, all of a sudden I realized there was no money coming in. One Saturday afternoon, I spent most of my last fifteen dollars in the supermarket, my checking account was down to a pittance and I couldn't get to the savings bank until Monday morning. I panicked because my kids and I were supposed to go to the movies with friends Sunday afternoon. I had to borrow money. I wasn't feeling too strong anyway and being without money makes you feel even more insecure and helpless. I went to my lawyer first thing Monday morning and he started a temporary support order. Fortunately, my husband mailed a check four days later."

Women can start support orders themselves through their local family courts or their equivalents. But actually getting support money in one's hands can take up to thirty days and then such an order is difficult to enforce. Many women have to rely on welfare until their support is regular.

From the moment a woman hears her attorney's fees, she realizes the important part money will play in her thinking from now on.

"I won't take a case unless a woman has some money

up front for a retainer, or, at the very least, owns a house or a condominium jointly with her husband," one Chicago lawyer told me. "I've been burned too many times when I've taken a case on speculation assuming the husband would cover legal expenses. Sometimes the judge doesn't award an attorney his full fee under those circumstances. Other times you have to wait so long to get paid, it's not worth it. And sometimes her husband never pays."

You and the children will still need to eat, buy shoes or go to the dentist, and have some spending money. Your husband will be less sympathetic to those needs when he's not under the same roof.

Since custody still goes to women in nine out of ten divorces and because women generally have less income and less access to money than their husbands, it is important that they get what is legally theirs.

"Know your expenses, know what you need to live," advises one lawyer. "Too many women are so anxious to get him out of the house that they settle for less than they're entitled to or than they need. And once the guy's living elsewhere with his own expenses and maybe a girlfriend, he's not going to come up with any more than he has to."

If You Have Custody—Father

If you are a man with custody of your children, money can help you feel physically and emotionally more secure.

Where you do have custody, the chances are likely that your wife is not contributing much or anything in the way of alimony, even if she is able to. (At this writing the divorce laws in many states make no mention of the possibility of alimony payments by a wife to a husband.)

If You Do Not Have Custody—Mother

While you probably will not be supporting your children, you may feel you want to provide them with whatever financial help you can afford in order to make their lives easier. (Tell them you're giving what you can—because you love them.) If your income is limited and you don't want to be tied down to a specific amount of child support, you can contribute in other ways. Give the children spending money when they visit you or pay for occasional extras—ice skates, a pottery class, soccer camp, ballet lessons. Contributing financially may be a sacrifice but knowing you're handling your responsibilities is important for your self-esteem.

If You Do Not Have Custody—Father

In the more typical case, you will not have custody of your children, but money still plays an important role. It is important to your children's sense of self-esteem and to your relationship with them that they know you are contributing whatever money you can to their support. Even though you are concerned about your children, you will probably have quite different concerns from your wife when you discuss money with your lawyer. If she does not work or does not earn as much as you do, you will want to provide fairly for your children. At the same time, you will resent having to come up with so much that you feel that you are giving your former wife a free ride. You pay for her rent, her utilities, your own rent and utilities, possibly one or two automobiles. You don't see the children as often as you'd like. And you work all the time—maybe even at two jobs.

You also have a new life to build. A new apartment to buy furniture for. You would like to have enough money left over to have some social life for yourself. No matter how carefully worked out a settlement is, everyone usually has to cut back. Two families and two households cannot live anywhere near as well on the income that had been supporting one family and one household. The Bureau of Labor Statistics estimates that it costs a single parent with two children *plus* another single person (the other spouse) 12 to 43 percent more to maintain the same standard of living as a couple living together with two children.

In exchange for your firm commitment of support, you should insist that your visitation rights be *precisely* spelled out. Too often, an angry woman will use the children to punish her husband or negotiate for a better settlement. Some women go as far as to try to sever the relationship between a child and his father. Your ex-wife may not be at home when you arrive to pick up your child, or telephone to say the children are busy with homework or are not feeling well when you were planning to see them.

Many fathers faced with this kind of constant frustration have given up the fight to see their children. Many others have ended up spending a great deal of money in court in order to have their visitation rights confirmed by a judge. Don't treat visitation as a casual thing. Be specific in your written agreement. For example, stipulate "Every Sunday from 9–9 and every Wednesday afternoon and overnight."

Working Out a Financial Settlement

Nancy and her husband, Peter, separated after eleven years of marriage and one child. For the final four years of their marriage, they had lived in Venezuela where Peter worked for an American company. When they separated, Nancy and her seven-year-old son, Anthony, moved back to Boston where Nancy had grown up. Peter stayed at his job in South America.

With the $750 a month Peter sent her (he earned $18,000 per year) Nancy could not get by. Averaged out on a monthly basis, the rent on her two-bedroom apartment was $425; utilities came to $65; food costs including groceries, school lunches and an occasional hamburger or pizza came to roughly $250; clothing, shoes, drugs and incidentals, another $75; and medical/dental costs, roughly $25—a total of $840—without any emergency or extraordinary expenditure (Nancy was going to need a car and Anthony's front teeth were already protruding and would need braces at some point). Nor did this take into account that Peter was paying most of the money as alimony rather than child support so that it was tax deductible for him. That meant that Nancy had to pay taxes on it.

Nancy's parents had lent her some money but were not able to afford very much. She needed a job. She found something with an insurance company. In two years she went from file clerk to assistant office manager of a small branch of an insurance company in a Boston suburb and is earning $10,000 a year. She has renegotiated her agreement with Peter who now pays her $250 per month in *alimony* and $500 a month in *child support* so that less of the money she receives is taxable to her. (See section in this chapter: *Tax Laws.*)

Nancy says she would like to buy a house and be able to give more to Anthony—piano lessons, perhaps overnight camp—but she doesn't have the money. She is considering opening a weekend catering business for weddings and parties on the side but she worries that anything taking more time away from Anthony would be a mistake especially since he so rarely sees his father.

Depending on the number and ages of children; the age, job history, and job prospects of the wife; the duration of a marriage; the income of husband and wife; and the amount of property between you; your lawyers, an accountant, and (as a last resort) a judge will put together a financial package including child support, alimony, if the less affluent parent has custody, and a division of property.

Rule number one: Don't discuss money with your spouse. That's what you're paying your lawyer to do and that's what he is trained to do. Let him do his job. If your spouse brings up money when you see him or talk to him on the telephone, just say your lawyer advised you not to discuss it and that he or she should get in touch with your lawyer. You will quickly find that nothing makes tempers flare like discussions over money. Avoiding them can keep a mother from going after every last cent she can get from her husband, or induce a father to be more generous when he agrees to a final settlement.

Where Fathers Are Self-Employed or Deal in Cash Businesses—A Mother's Concerns

Now that you know what you and the children need to live on, do you know what money, property, and other assets there are and how much of them you are entitled to? Your lawyer will want and need to know all the assets you and your spouse have between you.

If your husband is a teacher, an executive, or holds some other salaried job, has a jointly held bank account and stock account with you, and a life insurance policy naming you as beneficiary, it is not difficult to know his or her assets. But where he has his own business—a retail store, a law practice, a restaurant—or his own investment accounts; or is paid a significant part of his income in cash, as is a waiter, a cabdriver, an entertainer and others, you may not be aware of his full income and all of his assets.

Where you feel your husband may be concealing assets which you have no way of documenting, there are steps you can take to help your case and see to it that you get a fair settlement.

"My husband reported that he only took $20,000 out of his drycleaning business in personal income last year," said one woman who had been married fifteen years. "I knew that was well under what we really spent and my lawyer told me how I could show what was closer to his true income. He advised me to make a list of my own and my husband's expenditures as closely as I could remember them for the last six-month period that we lived together," she said. "How often we went to restaurants, plays, nightclubs, what our bills were at department stores, how often we entertained. He also advised me to include vacations we had taken, hotels we stayed at, and to state how often we buy new cars. This indicates true income or standard of living, he told me."

A New York matrimonial lawyer says, "Even if a man denies what his wife says they spend, she probably will have some receipts, some friends who went out with them or traveled with them, or even if it's her word against his, with a written record of dates, places, names, and times, the judge will place the burden of proof on him."

If your husband has a business or medical practice you may be entitled to a portion of it depending on the state you live in. This is usually handled with a payment spread out over a period of months or years.

A Father's Concerns

As a man who is self-employed or who receives much of his income in cash, you may well feel differently. Your income may be unpredictable. You may have a good year, followed by a slow year and may not want to be tied to a support figure based on an unusually successful year. Discuss this with your attorney.

One lawyer includes in the financial settlements of such a client a clause which gives the client the right to seek arbitration to try to have his support figure lowered if his income drops substantially. (The American Arbitration Association performs this service for less than $100—see Part 5, Chapter Twenty-Two.)

The Basic Question

How much will one of you have to pay and how much will the other receive?

In most states, the father is still considered primarily responsible for the support of his children. However, as more women work and accumulate assets, courts are reassessing this principle. In a recent case before the Brooklyn Appellate Division in New York State, *Carter vs. Carter*, the court ruled that an *automatic* presumption that a father must contribute more to the support of his children than his wife does is unconstitutional and that a wife's earnings, career potential and other circumstances must be examined.

However, if a woman does not work or works but earns very little and has few assets and her husband earns $20,000 or over, he will probably (although each case is different) end up paying roughly a third of his income in some combination of alimony and child support. A man earning roughly $25,000 to $35,000 will pay closer to half while a man earning over $40,000 will probably pay 50 percent of his income.

In setting support figures, judges often feel that if they set too high an amount, the man may fall behind in his payments or simply leave the state. This happens often. About 40 percent of all separated, divorced, or single women do not receive *any* assistance from the fathers of their children. Many others receive only small or erratic amounts of help. Few women can afford to take delinquent husbands to court except in those counties which provide such women with the free services of the county attorney's office to sue for back alimony or child support.

Experts agree that women, especially with children,

suffer a far greater decline than their husbands in their standards of living following a separation and divorce. Yet judges, aware that the courts cannot directly enforce their rulings, tend to set alimony and child support payments on the low side, thinking in terms of commitments which the men are most likely to live up to. As would be expected, those separated or divorced fathers in low-income groups generally contribute little to their families, while a high number of middle-income fathers— those earning over $15,000 per year—contribute more regularly. Among the very rich, financial settlements usually include generous alimony, child support, and property awards, the rationale being that there is no question of affordability and, where possible, a wife and children have a right to continue living at or near "the style to which they have become accustomed."

Waiting for the Settlement

While a financial statement is in the works, bills keep coming in. You won't want to pay large medical or other bills until you have to. On the other hand, you have to face your doctor, dentist, and local shopkeeper. You don't want to make them wait for months. As for large stores or other less personal debts, you should not jeopardize your credit rating, especially if you will be a woman alone, since credit will be hard to get. If you call those people whom you know personally and explain that you're waiting for final decisions as to who will be responsible for which debts, and ask your lawyer to write letters to department stores and such explaining the situation, they will generally be willing to be patient.

Alternatives to Lifetime Alimony

Alimony awards are becoming increasingly less common. More women work. As for those who do not the prevailing thought among lawyers and judges is that women, particularly those in their forties or younger who do not work, should start doing so, either immediately or after some training. This thinking has resulted in sensible alternatives to lifelong or nearly lifelong alimony awards, such as temporary alimony for two or three years to help a woman establish herself in a career or a large, one-time payment, known as "bulk" alimony.

"I have often suggested to men clients, that if they can swing it, they give their wives full possession of the house, the co-op, or some other lump sum, in exchange for a written promise never to ask for alimony payments. I've advised businessmen, dentists, a successful writer, and several other men who were earning in excess of $40,000 to do this," explained a matrimonial attorney. (Of course, if a man goes on to earn significantly more money after the divorce, his child-support payments can be increased.)

A one-time, bulk payment makes it easier for a man to start building his life again. It's good for the woman, too. She doesn't have to wonder from month to month, "Will he pay or won't he?"

"A man has to be careful, however, when he agrees to 'bulk' alimony," one lawyer warns, "to protect himself against his wife asking for more money later on. The only way he can legally protect himself is by being the *plaintiff* in the case and getting the divorce on fault grounds. Then if she goes out and spends all the money on a world cruise, she can't come back to him for more money."

255

Not long ago in the state of New York there was a young woman who had been divorced from her husband for a year. Because she had worked as a secretary during the years he was in medical school, she went to court asking for a judgment that her former husband should now pay for her tuition and expenses in the law school where she had just been accepted. She won.

Division of Property

The house, the car, the jewelry, the antiques, the stocks, the savings, and other valuable property will be divided between you and your spouse according to the laws in the state in which you live, unless, as in the discussion above, you, the husband, gave up your rights to certain properties by using them as part of your bulk alimony payment in exchange for not having to pay long-term alimony. There are many differences among the states on this issue. In some, property goes only to the person in whose name it is; but in most a woman's housework and contributions to a man's home and family life are considered qualifications for a roughly equal share in property. In still other states, those with community property laws, property acquired after the marriage, not by gift or inheritance, is divided fifty-fifty.

If there is to be alimony and/or child support, when does the more affluent parent, usually the man, have to begin paying? Many men send their families money immediately, without a legal order to do so. But technically, a man is not required to pay until there is a formal support order. This need not involve a long delay. A woman can have a temporary order started within a few days through her lawyer.

A support order protects both women and men. For a woman with children, a clearly spelled out support agreement, effective soon after the separation, guarantees her a regular income. She will not have to deplete the children's bank accounts, or borrow from her parents, sell her jewelry, if any, or apply for welfare. And while a legal support order obligates a man to pay a certain amount of money each week or month, it also protects him from surprises like a bill for $1,000 from a department store.

Tax Laws

There are certain laws that you should discuss with your attorney and an accountant in planning your financial settlement. Though you and your spouse may not see eye to eye on much at this point, you both will probably agree that you don't want to pay any more money to the IRS than is necessary. After discussing your finances with the professionals, you can decide how the following stipulations pertain to you:

1. Alimony is tax deductible by the person who pays: taxable to the person who receives. (A divorced man can deduct from his income tax many of his wife's and children's expenses—food, housing, utilities—which he could not do as a married man.) The greater the gap in tax brackets of husband and wife, the more sense it makes to call a major portion of your payment "alimony." ("There should be at least a 30 percent gap," says one attorney.) If a woman is starting a career, however, and the income gap will narrow, it will gradually work against her.

2. Child-support payments are tax-free to the recipient. They cannot be deducted by the person who makes them.

3. If one spouse agrees to pay mortgage, insurance premiums, orthodontic expenses, or private school tuition, this can be paid as alimony and deducted.

4. If a man transfers his home to a spouse, he will have to pay capital gains tax on it. If the house was owned jointly, he pays the tax on only half the profit. Capital gains taxes must be paid on some other assets such as stocks which have appreciated. It would make more sense for a man to transfer a $10,000 bank account than $10,000 worth of stock in American Telephone and Telegraph.

5. In the event the person paying alimony dies, the original settlement should stipulate that payments be continued from the estate and thus, if previously designated as such, escape estate taxes.

6. Because alimony stops if a woman remarries, if she is collecting the bulk of her support in alimony (to allow her husband to deduct it), she can protect herself by having a provision that her child-support payment will increase in the event that she remarries.

7. A parent can claim a child as a dependent as long as he pays $600 a year for support of the child, no matter how much the other parent is contributing. The current tax exemption is $750 per year, per child.

8. More important are medical expenses. Only the

parent who lists the child as a dependent can deduct medical expenses. However, a loophole in the tax law permits one parent, say the father, to add medical expenses to the lump sum he pays as alimony and deduct the total amount. If the mother claims the children as dependents, she can then issue the payments for medical costs and deduct them.

9. Legal fees for arranging alimony are tax deductible. Legal fees for tax advice are also deductible. Lawyers often arrange for one spouse to pay enough additional alimony (deductible) to cover the other's legal fees, but this kind of padding, if it's discovered, will be disallowed by the IRS.

10. You can now claim 20 percent or up to $400 of the babysitting costs for one child ($800 maximum for two or more) as a *tax credit*. A parent can claim these child care costs whether or not she is the parent who deducts that child as a dependent. (Remember, baby-sitting fees of $50 or more in any quarter of the calendar year are subject to Social Security taxes.)

11. File a "joint" return when paying your taxes until you are legally separated. That is the most advantageous status. The next best is "head of household" (for which you may be eligible. Check with an accountant) followed by "single," and last is "married, filing separately."

12. You can still take a standard deduction (without itemizing) *plus* an alimony deduction above the line (from your gross income). If you both agree to do so, you can renegotiate your settlement at any time to benefit from new tax laws. Experts

recommend including ."escalator" clauses in child-support and alimony figures in order to allow for cost-of-living increases and to avoid the $200 to $300 in legal fees usually involved in renegotiating an agreement.

You're on Your Own with the Children

The separation is legal. The twenty- to thirty-odd-page separation settlement is drawn up. The next stage of your life can begin.

Your children didn't want the separation. They will fight it and all the changes that accompany it and when you tell them that they will have to give up their music or tennis lessons and maybe even summer camp, they will surely resist it. It is important that you show them at the start that you are in charge. If you take a kind but firm position of "This is how it is, we'll manage," it will be better all around. If they're old enough, they might get part-time jobs to pay for some of the things they want or make up for the allowances they used to get. Learning that they can't have everything they want and that they're able to do things for themselves may be more beneficial to them than a $1,200 summer at camp.

Even though a basic financial arrangement has been signed, there is always room for some flexibility (and haggling) when it comes to money. It will remain a delicate issue, so you should learn to handle it diplomatically and coolly, if possible. While before your settlement, you could refer all money questions to your attorney, you're on your own now. If you want to bring up violin lessons or a camping trip to your former spouse, try not to be sarcastic or judgmental. Otherwise, the inevitable argument will develop and without thinking, you're liable to express your naked feelings within the children's earshot, "That creep won't even pay for camp." But it hurts your children to think their father doesn't care about them and it's probably not true. Without angry battles their father may be more inclined to stretch himself financially for them.

Try to discourage your children from "asking" for things every time they see Daddy. Though the budget may be tight, you don't want to raise manipulative children.

You're on Your Own Alone

You're probably not swimming in money and may have your own resentments. You're paying all the bills. Your ex has the kids (you may or may not be getting along with them at the moment). What probably runs through your mind is "Why doesn't she get a job?" One father explained his situation: "I live in a hundred-and-fifty-dollar-a-month furnished studio. Economically, this bothers me tremendously. There is so much more that I could do with the kids if I weren't paying her rent, her utilities and her food. It comes close to nine hundred dollars a month and it leaves me strapped."

As a visiting parent, at the same time, try to resist the temptation to give your children an abundance of toys and surprises to make up for not being with them more. Money is not equal to time and you probably wouldn't want them to think it is either. If it bothers you that you don't see them more, tell them so. That will probably mean more to them than a ten-dollar gift. And let your children know what you're contributing to their support, not with the tone "See what I'm doing for you," but rather, "I want you to know how much I love you and I'm giving your mother as much money as I can to help take care of you."

Your Future as a Custodial Parent

For a woman, going back to school or getting a job may be therapeutic steps toward her personal growth, her independence, regaining some of the self-confidence that most women say becomes so shaky during a separation and, most of all, toward financial independence. If it does these things, it will probably make you a better parent, too. The less you have to depend on your husband, who, statistics say, will very likely remarry relatively soon, the less entangled you will be with a relationship that should be behind you.

Because your children will be making so many major adjustments, you (or your husband, if one of you was at home more of the time) might wait a few months before actually going to work. You should check with your lawyer, as well, as to how any income you earn would affect your financial settlement and your tax status. Explore your options carefully—school, part-time work, full-time work, or some combination of those.

Following a separation, some women look for ways to lighten the bills, housework, baby-sitting (especially if they're going to school), and loneliness. Sharing a home with another mother with children is one solution, but it is not for everyone. It can make you complacent. With the relief from money worries and tedium it can provide, you

262

can become too comfortable with this arrangement when you should really be thinking about school or work and getting on with your own life. Think it through carefully and if you should share a home with someone, make certain that your new housemate is emotionally and financially reliable. You don't need any new burdens at this time.

Some single parents take in a boarder, often a student, to contribute a small amount to the rent, to help with some housework, and be there as a baby-sitter some of the time. "Just knowing that I can get out to the movies occasionally or see friends is a tremendous relief which having Jane in the house gives me," reported one mother who has an art student living in.

What is important here is not to make hasty decisions about changing your life in any drastic way. "Lie low is the best advice I can give," said one psychiatrist. "This is a time when you're not at your most stable. You might decide to do something that will upset your children and you even more. Give yourself some time before making any big decisions."

With some financial independence as well as some outside interests, women are less likely to feel the anger or frustration toward former husbands which comes from economic deprivation and can lead to some of the worst disasters of custody which will be discussed in the following chapter.

Chapter Twenty

CUSTODY DISASTERS

Most divorced parents are able to put their children's interests first. They control their need for revenge and their anger toward their former spouse. However, some are so embittered by the marriage and divorce experience that they cannot control their own worst instincts. And then there are those men and women who believe that their extreme behavior—violence; badmouthing the other parent; parents who no longer love each other or get along but continue living under the same roof; child-snatching; closing the other parent off from the children—is in the long-range interests of their children.

It is difficult to estimate the effects on children of such actions, but they definitely are harmful. They undermine the child's needs for stability and a continuing relationship with two parents.

Violence

It is sad and frightening for the adults involved, more so for the children, that the level of anger between two people who were once romantically attached to one another, engaged, married, and making plans to share a lifetime (including being happy parents) can escalate to a high level. The frustration, loss, and hurt that come with many divorces can, in an emotionally unstable person, actually endanger lives.

Stephanie, the wealthy New York mother of four-year-old Debbie, was worried that her ex-husband, from whom she had been divorced for two years, would take the child out of the country. He had threatened to take her to his native Italy. Although she had the child protected by a private detective, Stephanie was not satisfied and decided to have her husband killed.

The private detective she employed put her in touch with a "hit man" who agreed for $25,000 to abduct the man, force him into a car, drive to a nearby lake where he would shoot the husband, and sink his body in the lake.

Stephanie's plan might have succeeded had the hit man not panicked at the last minute and gone to the police. After secretly informing the husband of the situation, the hit man went through the motions of the planned killing and turned over to Stephanie a photograph of what appeared to be a dead body as well as her husband's wallet. She paid him the balance of the promised $25,000.

The police arrived soon after to arrest Stephanie.

Gene is just one example of the anger and the potential for violence often found in the aftermath of divorce. Gene, a New York City policeman, had been divorced for one year. One day, on his way to work in the subway, he was talking with Mario, a fellow officer who had just separated from his wife.

"Do you know what would have been better for me?" Gene asked his friend. "To shoot her. I do a year in jail. The kids stay with my mother. After a year, I've got them," he said in all seriousness. "And that arrogant, bastard lawyer of hers. I wanted to shoot him even more than her."

"My lawyer already has fifteen hundred dollars of mine and for what?" Mario beefed. "One hour in court and filling out a few papers."

"I'm going back to court to say I can't afford so much child support," Gene said, "as soon as she gets married. But you know what'll happen then?" he asked. "That bastard boyfriend of hers'll tell me, 'I'll adopt them,' and you know what? (pounding his fist) . . . *then* I'll shoot *him!*"

This kind of talk may have given Gene a chance to release some of his anger without harming anyone. Or it may actually incite him to violence. Forcing one's children to have to deal with a parent's criminal behavior is something that any clear-thinking parent would find abhorrent. Yet, it does happen because a parent's worst emotions sometimes get out of control. If people realized more about the potential for violence in divorce, it is hoped that, for the sake of their children who have been hurt enough, they might be more open to getting professional help rather than waiting until it is too late.

Badmouthing

There may be instances where your former spouse's behavior invites scorn or criticism, yet it is not helpful to your child to tell him that parent is "bad."

If your former wife drinks a little too much, chain smokes, and keeps a sloppy home, you might feel like telling your son, "Your mother is a disgusting person. She's filthy and lazy." But all that will do is make the child feel bad. It will make him feel inadequate if his mother is made to sound like a complete failure, and it will make him angry because his mother probably has some good points.

Most differences between divorced parents have two legitimate sides. A man may find his ex-wife flamboyant and loud; she may think him dull and boring. But this is not important, the marriage is over. The important point is that your child will resent you for stressing the negatives about his mother. And he will doubt his own worth. This is not good for the child. He must come to terms with whatever his mother is. And for that he needs you to support him rather than upset him.

Yet, in an extreme case should a parent pretend? Should he say, "When Mommy stays in bed all day and doesn't straighten up the house or bother with you, she really loves you," or "When Daddy slaps you, he doesn't mean it and he loves you?"

"Don't lie," says psychiatrist Dr. Sanger. "The child needs you to be understanding and compassionate yet truthful. Say, 'I'm sorry that when you bring friends to Mommy's, it's so messy there,' or 'I'm sorry Daddy hit you. He has problems controlling his temper.'" Your child needs you to help him understand what is actually going on around him—not to make things seem worse or better than they are.

Kenny's father disappointed him every Saturday. He was due to pick the boy up at ten on Saturday mornings, but he always called at ten-thirty or eleven to say he would be a few hours late or to cancel because of "business."

Kenny's mother would become furious, not only because she would have to change her plans at the last minute but because she knew Kenny was hurt. After referring to the boy's father on several occasions as a "no-good bum" and worse, she realized that her reaction was only making it worse for Kenny.

She sat down with him and said, "When we get angry or hurt, very often we exaggerate and say things that aren't true. Your father is definitely not a bum. He's not a bad person at all. He always sends us money on time. He took half of his vacation to go on a fishing trip just with you. He loves you very much but he can be unreliable. I will talk to him. And next time you ask him if the two of you can discuss your Saturday visits. Tell him that what he does is disappointing to you. Maybe if he's more aware of how you feel and how I feel, he'll try harder. You know, Kenny, none of us is perfect."

Estranged and Living Under the Same Roof

There are those couples who no longer get along and have agreed officially or unofficially that they will separate who continue living in the same house. They generally occupy different parts of the house, or at least have separate bedrooms. They may say they are doing it for financial reasons ("It's too expensive to maintain two households"), or for the children ("This way, we both get to see them"), or because each wants the house and/or the children and doesn't want to abandon what he considers to be his.

In fact, experts say, the root of this behavior by parents is usually not financial nor is it for the children but, as was discussed earlier, usually comes from a need to hang on to the relationship in some way. "Usually they can't give up the fighting," says one psychiatrist. At this point the parents need some professional help to get them to take the next step, if only so the children can get some consistency into their lives.

As for the children, on the surface this arrangement doesn't necessarily seem to be a bad idea, provided the parents can keep from throwing pots at each other. But it is a bad idea. At best it is unwise; at worst, destructive.

It gives children a confusing message. Parents are apart but together. Children wonder, what is the reality? Are they getting back together? Is one going to leave? This situation only prolongs the anxiety of something definite, and, above all, children need to know who is going to leave and when—something they can count on.

Children's imaginations are extremely active. Most children of separation or divorce wish their parents would get back together. This kind of situation makes it difficult for them to accept the reality that the marriage is over, put their fantasies to rest, and get on with their lives.

Child-snatching

Child-snatching connotes bizarre and unusual behavior. Most people would be startled to learn that there are 100,000 cases a year in the United States of abducting one's own child or children without legal sanction. It is one of the most harmful consequences of divorce which children suffer.

On Monday morning while walking the fifty yards from their house to the school-bus stop, Margaret and Catherine were startled by a voice calling their names. When they turned they saw a blue station wagon driving slowly along. Their father was slouched down in the back seat and a man they had never seen before was driving.

"There are my two favorite girls," their father called out the window. "Come on, let's go for a ride." The two girls, eleven and nine, willingly climbed into the car.

The girls were thankful that their father had brought snacks of cookies and fruit because they drove until well after lunch time. They had asked their father several times where they were going. He only told them, "Never you mind. Daddy will take care of you."

Exactly eight months later, a private investigator who specialized in locating children who have been "snatched" by a parent, found Catherine and Margaret living in an isolated farmhouse several states away.

The detective notified the girls' mother and informed her that the girls were attending school in a nearby town. The mother arrived in the town, observed her daughters from afar for three days. On the fourth day, she was waiting outside the school building at twelve-thirty, the time Margaret's and Catherine's classes came out to play in the yard following their lunch.

The girls were surprised and confused when they saw their mother, but after some discussion, they agreed to come with her. From that point on, a woman bodyguard hired by their mother accompanied them everywhere.

The girls hadn't been kidnapped because the law specifically exempts the taking of a child by one of his parents. The term used for this act is "snatching." Margaret and Catherine had been "snatched" and their mother could not get the police to help her. "When we find out it's a parent that has the kid, then it becomes a child-custody dispute and we get right out of it" is the way one police lieutenant explained their position.

Custody laws vary from state to state. A parent who disagrees with a decision or dislikes a custody arrangement in one state can move his or her child to another state without fear of serious legal recrimination. This, the parent hopes, will accomplish one of two results:

1. He or she will get a new trial in the state he moved to and might find a judge who agrees with him, or

2. He or she will live with the children in secret for an extended period of time (often for a year or more), at which point a judge may decide that while the children legally belong in the custody of their other parent, it would hurt the children still further to break the close "psychological" relationship they have now formed with this parent. Should the judge rule that the children be returned to their custodial parent from whom they have now grown apart, they will have serious difficulty readjusting. And they will have suffered two wrenching separations. It is difficult to imagine a situation in which child-snatching could truly be considered in the best interest of the child.

A group called Children's Rights, Inc., was recently formed in Washington, D.C., to counsel and advise parents whose children have been "snatched" and to help in the children's recovery.

The practice of abducting one's own children from the home of the children's custodial parent is unconscionable.

Yet, with over 100,000 child-snatching cases each year, it clearly continues uncontrolled in those forty-three states which have not adopted the Uniform Child Custody Act. This law provides that states which ratify it will honor and enforce all custody decisions of all other participating states and hold any parent in contempt who violates the law. As additional states decide to adopt the Uniform Child Custody Act, fewer children will be subjected to the upsetting, uprooting ordeal.

Separating a Child from His Parent

Another of the tragic outcomes of divorce and custody is cutting a child off from one parent by means other than snatching. This happens where one parent moves a great distance away without informing the other parent. The many reasons this hurts a child are discussed in Chapter Eleven on Part-Time Parents. But a major one is that the child will fantasize that the absent parent is a hero or villain and will not know what the reality is.

Divorced . . . Again

There are those children who go through the disintegration of their families not once, but twice and three times. Some call it serial marriage, but to children it is always multiple divorce. For some children, it seems to become easier each time. The first time is the hardest. Then they cope better with each successive divorce.

Vanessa, at ten, had lived in three full-time homes and had regularly "visited" three others. Both her parents were on their third marriages. Yet, Vanessa functioned well in school, with her many friends and with her family, including her mother, her father, her stepparents—all four of them and numerous stepbrothers and stepsisters.

Vanessa, however, had something special, something which psychiatrists say can help such a child. She had always been exceptionally close to her maternal grandmother, with whom she used to live for months at a time each time her mother was divorced.

The children who cope well with their parents' repeated divorces are the minority of cases and generally there's someone in the background who's stable—a grandparent, an aunt. Other children are shaken by the constant instability in their lives. Many of them use drugs, fail in school, and generally don't seem to care about themselves.

Jered was sixteen when his mother married John—his mother's third husband and his second stepfather.

In spite of the many parents and stepparents in Jered's life, it seemed that no one had much time for him or took an interest in him. Each of his parents and former stepparents had remarried. Some had new families. Others had children by an earlier marriage. John, his latest stepfather, was a successful and busy executive who wanted Jered's mother to travel and entertain with him a great deal, so they were often out or away and Jered was home alone.

When Jered spent the summer with his father in Texas as he normally did, he often found it embarrassing and sexually stimulating to be around his new twenty-eight-year-old stepmother who spent most summer days in a bikini suit at their backyard pool.

Much to the surprise of Jered's parents, he announced

274

after the summer that he wasn't going back to prep school for his senior year. "Why should I bother?" he said.

Jered's grades had been dropping over the previous two years and his parents eventually learned that he had tried many different drugs. "Once," a friend reported to Jered's mother some time later, "Jered told me he had left some hash out on his dresser just to see if he could get you to notice. But I guess you didn't."

Jered has had a series of part-time jobs, but at this point says he is not going back to school.

Because these children are exposed to more potential trauma than most, they should, as a preventive measure, probably be seen by a highly competent psychiatrist or psychologist to allow them to discuss the emotional jolts they have lived through.

The children themselves express various reactions to parents' decisions to divorce . . . again.

One twelve-year-old boy whose father married for the fourth time and whose mother was on her third husband said, "I know that when I get married, I'm not going to get a divorce. It'll just be me, my wife and my kids. I won't do this to them."

A thirteen-year-old girl whose parents had six marriages between them, when asked how she felt about her parents' divorces, said with a shrug, "Oh, it doesn't bother me," but then admitted sadly, "That's not really true. I'm just glad I'm getting out of here and going to boarding school."

PART FIVE

WHERE TO GET HELP WHEN YOU NEED IT

Chapter Twenty-One

DON'T BE SURPRISED IF THERE ARE PROBLEMS

"We have not encountered a victimless divorce," says one experienced divorce researcher.

In almost every family of divorce, someone suffers emotionally. There are those to whom the stress is debilitating.

Sixteen percent of American children have divorced parents. But of all children referred for psychiatric evaluations in their schools, 33 percent are children of divorce. These children are more likely than others to develop problems. The symptoms which lead to their referrals include: extreme aggressiveness, poor schoolwork, depression and loneliness, phobias, stealing, drug use, and others.

Psychiatrists and psychologists who work with families of divorce say that children who have trouble adjusting usually have parents who aren't adjusting well—men and women who haven't gotten over their guilt, their anger, their resentment, or their sadness over the divorce. Or those who just can't cope with the stresses of managing a family and being unmarried.

There are many mothers, fathers, and children in divorced families who could be leading happier, more successful lives than they are at the moment. Sometimes it is just a matter of being able to talk to people with similar concerns. In other cases, group or individual counseling or psychotherapy can help a person make enormous strides in the way he manages his life, including (and importantly) his children.

Following are suggestions for handling a range of practical and psychological problems you or your children might face following the breakup of your marriage.

Chapter Twenty-Two

REACHING AN AGREEMENT YOU CAN LIVE WITH

Custody, visitation rights, child support, and similar details of a separation agreement can often make husband, wife, and attorneys, who may have been on the brink of signing the papers, angry and vindictive all over again. Or disagreements over the same issues may arise after a separation agreement or divorce is final, again arousing old arguments and hurting parents and children. All members of a family are better off if they reach an agreement that each feels comfortable with and can stick to.

The American Arbitration Association, a public service, nonprofit organization with offices in cities across the country, is set up to handle many kinds of disputes—for labor, business, families, and others. For families, they have impartial experts—mediators, referees, and arbitrators with training in settling disagreements—training

281

lawyers generally do not have—to help families of separation and divorce with the emotional issues of custody, visitation, and finances. The AAA experts work along with attorneys for the purpose of reaching a fair and prompt agreement.

AAA mediators, referees, and arbitrators have somewhat different powers and each is appropriate for specific situations or problems. A *mediator* makes recommendations on issues necessary to complete a separation agreement. A *referee* is called in to decide issues which a couple cannot resolve and which are necessary to the agreement. And an arbitrator, after holding hearings, makes a binding judgment on any disputes which arise over custody, visitation, or financial issues *after* the separation agreement has been signed.

If you are having trouble resolving custody, visitation or money matters either before or after you have signed your separation agreement, contact your nearest American Arbitration Association office, explain your situation in detail, and they will advise you what they can do for you and what your next step should be, depending on whether you will be applying for mediation, decision by referee, or arbitration. At this writing, thirty-five states have modern arbitration laws which provide for the enforcement of AAA decisions. On the subject of custody, some judges feel that disputes are best handled through the AAA. Others feel that a full trial is the only way to provide a complete hearing. Depending on your state law, and the judge who handles your case, you may or may not be able to submit custody matters to the AAA. Some regional offices of the AAA are:

BOSTON, Richard M. Reilly; 294 Washington Street; Boston, Mass.

CHARLOTTE, John A. Ramsey; 3235 Eastway Drive; Charlotte, S.C.

CHICAGO, Charles H. Bridge, Jr.; 180 N. LaSalle Street; Chicago, Ill.

CINCINNATI, Philip S. Thompson; 2308 Carew Tower; Cincinnati, Ohio

DALLAS, Helmut O. Wolff; 1607 Main Street; Dallas, Texas.

LOS ANGELES, Tom Stevens; 2333 Beverly Boulevard; Los Angeles, Calif.

MIAMI, Joseph A. Fiorillo; 2451 Brickell Avenue, Miami, Fla.

NEW YORK, Robert E. Meade; 140 West 51 Street; New York, N.Y.

PHILADELPHIA, Arthur R. Mehr; 1520 Locust Street; Philadelphia, Pa.

PHOENIX, Paul A. Newnham; 222 North Central Avenue; Phoenix, Ariz.

ROCHESTER, Theodore S. Kantor; 36 West Main Street; Rochester, N.Y.

SAN FRANCISCO, William B. Allender; 690 Market Street; San Francisco, Calif.

SEATTLE, Neal M. Blacker; 810 Third Avenue; Seattle, Wash.

WASHINGTON, Garylee Cox; 1730 Rhode Island Avenue, N.W.; Washington, D.C.

Chapter Twenty-Three

COPING WITH DIVORCE AND CUSTODY

It's dinnertime. The kids are fighting. You're tired from working all day and you're taking your second drink because you feel you can't cope without it.

Or, you need information—on how to prepare a resume, on getting a lawyer, on housing, on day care, or on applying for welfare benefits.

You are a parent living alone with children. Sometimes you need professional advice in handling a specific problem. Other times you need someone to talk to, to blow off steam to. Getting this kind of help when you need it can help you survive.

There are many organizations, courses, newsletters, and telephone counseling services to serve the single parent. A large number are publicly or privately funded and subsidize a range of services from psychological counseling for parents and children to weekly lectures on topics important to single parents to weekend family camping trips.

Following are some of the major organizations, newsletters, and other opportunities aimed at helping separated and divorced parents and their children:

Catalyst. 14 E. 60 Street; New York, N.Y. 10022. Nonprofit organization working directly with women; local resource groups that are concerned with *women and employment.*

Center for Children in Family Crisis. 1603 Arrott Bldg,; 401 Wood St.; Pittsburgh, Pa. (412) 281-0552. Creative program for children and parents focusing on changes of divorce.

Creative Divorce National Counseling Center. 818 Fifth Avenue; San Rafael, Calif. 94901. Groups for adults, children, research, education, training center for divorce counseling.

Displaced Homemakers Alliance. 4223 Telegraph Avenue; Oakland, Calif. 94609. Interested in *women returning to work.*

Divorce and Marital Stress Clinic. 1925 N. Lynn Street; Suite 800; Arlington, Va. 22209. Walk-in counseling, seminars, support groups.

Family Mediation Center, Inc. 291 Lindbergh Dr. N., Atlanta, Ga. 30305. Private center.

George F. Doppler, Coordinator, National Council of Marriage and Divorce Law Referee and Justice Organizations. P.O. Box 60; Broomall, Pa. 19008. Provides list of *organizations for men, fathers' rights.*

MOMMA. P.O. Box 567; Venice, Calif. 90291. Program similar to Parents Without Partners but smaller.

North American Conference of Separated and Divorced Catholics. The Paulist Center; 5 Park Street; Boston, Mass. 02108. Newsletter, $7/year.

Parents and Child Care Resources. 1855 Folsom Street; San Francisco, Calif. 94103. Referral services, day care information hot line.

Parents Without Partners, Inc. 7910 Woodmont Avenue; Washington, D.C. 20014. With over 130,000 members, the largest organization devoted to single parents and their children. Educational materials, 900 chapters, magazine.

Single Parent Program, Family Service of Santa Monica. 1539 Euclid Street; Santa Monica, Calif. 90904. Cooperates with UCLA in excellent single parent program, group meetings, seminars.

Single Parent Resource Center. 105 East 22 Street; New York, N.Y. 10010. New center for New York area.

Sisterhood of Black Single Mothers. P.O. Box 155; Brooklyn, N.Y. 11203. Newsletter (25¢ a copy), support programs, day care, meetings, bibliographies. Hoping to expand to other areas of the country.

Women in Transition. 4634 Chester Avenue; Philadelphia, Pa. 14143. Excellent programs and publications, holds small group discussions, has telephone counseling. Is funded.

Most YM-YWCA's and YMHA's run groups for single parents as do some PTA's and local colleges.

Help for Yourself

After her separation, Mary spent most mornings on the telephone telling her family and friends that she had sacrificed the best part of her life for her no-good, ungrateful husband. She had depleted most of the nine thousand dollars she had from an inheritance in one court case and other legal fees in efforts to get more money from him and, in her words, simply to "get the bastard." Instead of completing her training in physical therapy as she had planned and getting on with the future, Mary was wasting months of her life, her energies, and her money. Because she was angry.

Walter spent more time with his children after his divorce than he ever had when he was married. During the half of each week they spent with him, he was home whenever they were—when they arrived home from school, he was there; if one was sick and couldn't go to school, he stayed home from the office that day. He not only lavished attention on them, but also gifts and large allowances. After a while, the small direct-mail advertising business which he ran was losing clients who were used to his personal attention. His children became fresh and more demanding. Walter felt guilty. But he showed his guilt by overindulging his children and sacrificing his business and personal life. To no one's advantage.

Anger and guilt and other strong emotions can stand in the way of your making a successful transition from being married to being single and can hurt your relationship with your children too.

Often talking with a psychiatrist, psychologist or family counselor experienced in helping families of divorce, can

288

help you get over the feelings that are keeping you from moving on—such as the conflict and frustration you may feel between your sense of responsibility to yourself and to your children, or what was wrong with your marriage and what you can do to avoid getting into the same kind of relationship again.

Psychiatrists, psychologists, and family counselors can be in private practice or work for mental health or social service agencies. They generally run both individual and group sessions, some groups being made up exclusively of separated and divorced people. In choosing a therapist, counselor, or agency, the most important thing you should look for is someone who has had experience and success in helping individuals and families going through divorce. Ask friends of yours who might know, your family doctor, your lawyer, or someone in the psychiatry department at a large hospital. Don't be discouraged if you have to wait for an appointment at an agency. They usually charge graduated fees and are generally busy. Ask for the earliest possible appointment. Call back periodically to ask if there are any openings because of cancellations and to remind them that you are still interested.

Chapter Twenty-Four

HELP FOR YOUR CHILD

Children whose parents are divorced are twice as likely as other children to be referred in their schools for psychiatric counseling. (These children are also more than likely to come from low-income homes so their problems are not due strictly to divorce.) Nevertheless, many children from lower-, middle-, and upper-income families of divorce may fail in school, become unusually aggressive, have phobias or other nervous symptoms, use drugs, get seriously depressed, and have other problems.

Many children of divorce are confused and troubled by guilt, like the boy who said, "Once I said I wanted to live with Mommy. That means I can't like Daddy anymore."

Others are angry. "My father left us. I don't ever want to see him again" is the way one boy felt.

Still others have trouble coping, "Sometimes Mom tells me her problems. But I don't know what to do about them," explained a ten-year-old girl.

Very often, these children need someone to talk to who understands how they feel. Their parents may not be the ones to do it because they themselves are under too much stress. A trained and objective professional probably has more chance at success. Child psychiatrists, child psychologists, or social workers trained to work with children can be in private practice or work for mental health or social service agencies. School psychologists and some guidance counselors may be able to help a child or will refer you to someone who can.

In the meantime, parents will be doing their children a service by getting on with their lives. As parents become more relaxed, happier, and busier, children will too.

PART SIX

THE FUTURE
OF YOUR FAMILY

Chapter Twenty-Five

LOVERS AND CHARMING STRANGERS
(Custody/Visitation and Dating)

Getting into the swing of dating is terribly important, but can be difficult for a newly separated person still carrying the emotional baggage of a marriage gone bad, concern for the children's adjustment, and the normal trepidations about meeting new people. How you handle this early period of your separation will very much affect your children's emotional well-being and your effectiveness as a parent.

Getting Started

"Dating! It sounds so silly for someone who's been married for sixteen years to talk about dates."

It had been almost six months since Joan had sex, in fact, since she had spent any time with a male, outside of her nine-year-old son and her father, who stopped by every so often.

"I hadn't really thought much about it until now. I didn't care about going out. Now, I'd sort of like to but I guess I'm afraid," Joan told her therapist, "and don't forget, Cathy is fourteen. I don't want to give her the wrong idea. It's confusing."

"It is confusing," the psychologist agreed. "But won't you be giving Cathy the wrong ideas if you are cloistered at home and don't go out with men?"

Staying home can become comfortable in a way and safe from new disappointments. But it's not the place to grow. And it can make you dependent on your children to the point that they worry about you, can't concentrate on their schoolwork, or feel guilty if they have good times with their friends. One mother told me how she realized what she was doing to her children. "Since our separation, the kids had had a good relationship with their father. Every Saturday he was there ready to take them to the zoo, to the park to play baseball, or home to make spaghetti. He was terrific with them and they always looked forward to their time with him. But one Saturday, after the girls had left, I found my son Robert, who was eleven at the time, still in his room. 'What are you doing home?' I asked him. 'Didn't you say your father had tickets to the hockey game at the college?'

" 'Yeah,' he said. 'But I called Dad last night and told him I wasn't going. I know you've been feeling lonely, Mom, and I just didn't want to leave you alone for the weekend.'

"At that point, I realized that I had better try to do something about myself. I started by joining a duplicate bridge group and I'm sharpening up my office skills for a job search. Then I decided to go along with my friend,

Marian, to a divorce counseling group she's been going to. It's not easy but I think we're all feeling better."

Remember the Children

Because your social life will probably reflect the "stages" of divorce discussed in Chapter 9, you can expect it to proceed in fits and starts with some mistakes and misjudgments. You might wonder how much of what you do during this time you should reveal to your children.

Whether they live with you or visit you, they will immediately wonder about anyone they think you're interested in: Will it mean that Daddy won't be with us as much? that now I'll have someone who will take me fishing? that Mommy will move away with her new boyfriend? that it's all right to sleep with someone on the second date? that it's all right to be sleeping with three people at the same time?

While it's healthy for separated men and women to risk new social involvements, consider your children's need for security.

No matter how you're feeling, your children are more vulnerable than you are. They have to be your first priority. The environment you provide, hours you keep, the people you spend time with, and what you do—even if it's only hinted at—will concern and affect their development.

Following many years of marriage which usually included a relatively conservative sex life, then a depressingly cold period around the time of the separation, many women and men begin what Nora, a mother of two, called "the experimental stage," which generally

297

amounts to testing the waters—trying out a few partners, exploring new techniques, and rediscovering the flirtation, dating, and sexual aspects of being single.

Yet many run into the problem that being single today is not so much a *re*discovery as a *new* discovery. If you were married for more than a few years, you may see little resemblance to the way it was the first time. Styles have changed. While today's casual attitude toward sex takes away a good deal of the tension in a relationship, it can make some people feel they're being pushed into something they're not ready for. Not ready to explain to their children either.

While not typical, one woman described her sexual activities for the year and a half following her separation as "The wilder the better!"

Some people have found that they had difficulty handling the lack of structure in their lives and that the wildness got out of hand. They would go out every night, pick up and sleep with people they hardly knew and simply go too far.

"For a while, I had lost interest in my children, my job, everything," explained a recently separated man. "Except making new conquests. I had to prove something to myself."

One woman reported being knocked down, kicked, and robbed in a hotel room by a man whom she had met and spent two hours with in a bar.

There are still other problems which the newly divorced may encounter in their effort to fit into single society. Particularly in the early stages of divorce, which may be the most sexually active in the life of a formerly married person, there is the very real threat of venereal disease.

Surprisingly, in spite of the availability of penicillin,

numerous VD clinics, and nationwide staffs of trained personnel, the number of cases of venereal diseases is rising rapidly.

The real enemies are apathy, ignorance, and fear. As one doctor put it, "If you have VD, you're not bad, you're sick." With any suspicious symptoms (genital discharge, pain; rash or sores in genital area, on fingers, hips or breasts; or flulike illness or swollen joints) see your family doctor or gynecologist or go to a public health clinic. Do the same if you suspect there is any possibility that you have been exposed, *particularly if you are a woman.* Frequently women show no symptoms until there is severe and permanent damage. Often a laboratory test is the only accurate method of diagnosing.

Out of concern for their children's feelings, most parents realize that it is best to keep *all* early experimental relationships out of the house and out of the children's lives.

But what happens after? After what amounts to a "crazy" period for some and a "hibernation" period for others? If you've had a crazy period, you will probably have calmed your hectic pace. If, on the other hand, you've been in "hibernation," you may, after a few months, have taken yourself by the hand, left the security of your four walls, and slowly begun meeting and trusting members of the opposite sex, perhaps even one person. Now how should you combine your social life with your parenting? Should the children meet all your dates? If not, which ones? How much time should you all spend together? How much should the children know about the sexual aspects of your relationships?

The experts who talked about custody for this book and have treated and counseled families of divorce agree that when it comes to dating, parents should keep several things in mind. First, because children of divorce easily worry that they might suffer further losses, they can resent you spending time without them and secretly think that you don't want them around. When you go on a casual date, it might be easier for your child to accept if you just say that you are "going out with friends."

Beware of Charming Strangers

Dr. Sanger gives another reason for keeping casual dates out of your child's life. "Some adults get along better with children than others," he explains. Any child, particularly one who lives with a single parent and may feel more needy for relationships with adults, can take a liking to a charming personable date you bring home. You may not care that much for the person or hardly know him. Yet, on his best behavior, your date may joke, play games, and build rapport with your child. If he doesn't appear again, your child may be very disappointed.

Something More Serious

When you're involved in what might be a serious relationship, your children should get to know the person. You will want to spend a good deal of your time both with your children and with your new companion, so take some excursions together—to parks, ball games, movies, museums, or restaurants. "Bob and I have been spending so much time together that the boys would feel left out if we didn't do some things together. Besides, I want to see how they all get along," one mother of twin boys told me.

If you see the possibility developing of a long-term relationship or marriage, you will want to know how your friend gets along with children and how your children feel about him or her.

Some parents, because they're anxious for things to go well, will interfere in the chemistry between their children and their new friend. "Don't talk too much when Diane is here," or "When Bill comes over, I want you to play one piece on the piano and go to bed," are the kinds of things they say.

Most parents say they have found, sometimes through their own mistakes, that it's best for all concerned to let things flow naturally. "People are usually on their best behavior anyway when they don't know someone well," explained one father. "I realized that by overcontrolling my children when they were with Maggie, I couldn't get an idea of how they would get along under normal circumstances. Because my children's happiness is my biggest responsibility now, I just decided to let things happen. They had plenty of disagreements, but now they respect each other and even seem to like each other. I learned a lot about Maggie too that I hadn't known before, just by staying in the background for a while."

Experts point out something else which you might want to consider here. Following your separation, your child may be concerned about his future, insecure about how much his parents really love him, and at least a bit guilty that he contributed in some way to the breakup.

If you make him feel that he has to be "liked" by an outsider in your life, that it's not good enough for him to be himself, you are only reinforcing those fears.

Sex and the Dating Parent

Parents whose children live with them and even those whose children visit regularly, find they have to plan their social lives around the children's schedules. Most parents have had moments when they resented the fact that they couldn't be as spontaneous as they were when they were single and without children and free to go out whenever they felt like it. Indeed, many parents find it best to limit much of their dating to the times the children's other parent has them. Or if they invite dates to come to their homes, they try to make it after they know the children will be asleep.

Most parents date and, at some point, their children become aware of it. Understandably, parents are concerned about handling sex in a way that will not upset or confuse their children.

Most professionals I spoke with felt that having sleep-over dates disregards children's feelings, what they sense is right and wrong, and may be overstimulating to them. While the times are becoming more liberal each day, most preteen-age children still see sex as being serious and usually confined to marriage. Teen-agers, on the other hand, need different considerations. As mother (or father) is making love on the other side of a closed door, the teen-age boy or girl probably finds it sexually stimulating. He or she may also feel they can take the same liberties with dates, or, because they resent what they see as their parents' promiscuousness they may, out of their disrespect, become overly rebellious.

"Keep sexuality out of children's lives," advises one child psychiatrist, who went on to talk about ten-year-old Brian. "His mother had moved out to live with her

302

boyfriend, leaving the boy in the custody of his father. When his mother wanted Brian to visit and spend time with her and her boyfriend, the boy went but was secretly outraged. He told me 'I hate that man she lives with. He's a bad influence on my mother.' "

Again, most parents say that their relationships with their children have fewer problems where: (1) They don't display their lovers, (2) they don't have dates sleeping over when the children are in the house, and (3) they don't take the children out with casual dates—out with friends, yes, dates, no. They feel it's a price and a responsibility of being a parent.

However, when relationships do become deep and serious, the situation often changes. A recent study indicates that 75 percent of divorced fathers have their steady girlfriends sleeping over some or all of the time, including times they have their children, although most admit to feeling some concern about what their children (and former wives) might do or think.

"It's worked out fine for us," Phil, a marketing manager for a pharmaceutical company told me. "When the children are here for their half of the week, we all do our share of the housework, cooking, and so on. I think the fact that Maryann has shown that she's interested in Paul and Louise, that she plays with them—and even sews clothes and makes things for them—has made them much more accepting of the affection I give her and of the fact that they know we sleep together."

Sex as a Weapon

Occasionally, a still angry parent will try to use a parent's sexual activities against him or her in an effort to win custody of a child. This can happen the first time custody is being decided or at a later time, to reopen a custody case.

"Be discreet," advised one judge. "It's best for the children and can prevent sex from being used as an issue in custody. If a parent is wild or very promiscuous, it's not going to look good for him."

Living Together

Cohabitation, or living together but not being married, wouldn't raise any but the most conservative eyebrows today, particularly in light of the alarming divorce statistics.

"If it's a decent relationship, I see no problem regarding the children," says New York State Supreme Court Judge Bentley Kassal.

Most judges and psychiatrists feel that a couple living together, providing the stability and warmth considered necessary to any child's healthy development, is not harmful.

Cohabitation, the Courts, and Custody

A number of recent judicial rulings have rejected the fact of cohabitation, sometimes referred to as "living in sin," as grounds for a change in custody.

One midwestern judge in a case where a father, who had custody of his children and had been living with a woman for a year was being sued by his former wife on the grounds that his conduct was immoral, stated, "The court is asked to disrupt the children because of their parents' changing social life . . . one must certainly question the relative morality of multiple marriages as opposed to informal living arrangements.''

And in a similar case in another state, this one where a father was challenging a mother's right to custody because she was living with a man to whom she was not married, the judge explained that a determination of custody does not depend on whether the court approves or disapproves of a parent's way of living, ''but whether the child is best located with the mother and there well-behaved and cared for.''

Try to Lead a Normal Life

Following divorce, it is best for parents and children to be active and involved in the outside world. For parents, this includes having a social life. It will be complicated this time around. More planning, more conflicts, and more sacrifice. But experienced parents say that things work themselves out and new routines develop. ''The kids got used to my going out,'' said one mother, ''just as they got used to my going out when I was still married to their father. It was hard in the beginning because we were getting adjusted to the divorce. Now it's easier.''

The Next Step

Most children learn to cope with and accept their parents' dating and even living with someone. But many are concerned about the next step. Will my mother or father get married again?

Remarriage will be part of the custody experience of roughly 90 percent of the children of divorce. It will complicate the lives of all the parents and children involved in it, but if it is handled well, it can make everyone happier and more secure.

Chapter Twenty-Six

REMARRIAGE AND CUSTODY
(Getting in Step)

The Family of the Future

Experts predict that nearly half of all couples married in the 1970s will divorce. Yet, five out of six divorced men and four out of five divorced women will remarry. If these statistics are correct, the "blended" family (also called the "remarried" or "reconstituted" family) is likely to become the most common family arrangement—more common than either the original nuclear family or the single-parent family.

While the original nuclear family has been undergoing unprecedented upheavals in past years—and in a recent profile of American families conducted by Zaida Giraldo and Jack Weatherford of the Center for the Study of the Family and the State at Duke University, the researchers state, ". . . the 'ideal' family . . . will never return as a significant force in American life"—other family forms are going strong. With the remarriage rate as an indication, no one is giving up on the family. Almost two-thirds of all couples remain married until death, and of those who divorce, 75 percent of the women and 83 percent of the men remarry in less than three years. And, surprising to most people, the very latest preliminary statistics indicate that *our divorce rate may be leveling off*, getting down to roughly a 2 percent increase in the past year or two as compared with an almost 12 percent annual average increase over the preceding several years.

As one psychiatrist commented on the idea that the family may be obsolete, "If the family ended, someone would reinvent it."

Inevitable Conflicts

This is not to say that remarriage is easy. It is usually more complicated. Her children. His children. Her ex-husband. His ex-wife. Stepbrothers and stepsisters. There are so many adjustments in most remarriages that people going into one usually can't help thinking, "If it didn't work the first time when it was just him, me, and our children, how can it possibly work this time?"

Money is another obstacle. The average cost as of 1979 of raising a child to the precollege age of eighteen is roughly $55,000. In a remarried family, there are often several children to raise.

Remarriage, where there are stepchildren, is strewn with emotional obstacles. Experts have said a realistic expectation for a man or woman going into the role of stepparent is "a truce," in Dr. Sanger's words. "The children may or may not get along with one another or with their stepparents. They may feel afraid that the interloper might make their situation worse. Yet Sanger believes that they secretly want to feel loved and hope it will work out. They feel a conflict there. Stepparents can either ease the conflict or add to it.

"A mistake some unrealistic stepparents make is trying to 'outdo' the natural parent," says one psychiatrist. "Kids will sense that you're really telling them, 'I don't like the way you do that' or 'the way your other parent taught you that. I do it this way,' and they'll resent it. Don't *ever* try to compete with their natural parent. In fact, in the long run everything will work out best if you do nothing to stand in the way of their relationship with their natural mother or father. That relationship is good for them, so it will be good for you."

When a parent has custody of his or her children for a large part of the time, whether in an exclusive- or a joint-custody arrangement and marries a man or woman without children, that custodial parent faces the unique pressures involved in trying to please the people whom he loves most, yet who may, at times, have conflicting interests.

He or she wants his children, who have suffered through more than their share of shock and uncertainty, to have a happy family life.

There is also the new spouse to think of. Having "failed" at a first marriage makes one doubly anxious to make the next one work, to see the other person's point of view, to be reasonable, helpful, and understanding.

There are bound to be clashes. One forty-year-old father explained, "Sometimes it's a double bind. The kids give my new wife a hard time because they still resent the divorce. I want to help her establish her authority but I don't want to be too hard on the kids because I know what they're going through. It's hard. I can see her problem too. She puts in all this effort and she doesn't get much thanks."

Another couple echoed similar. problems. Max, divorced with no children, married Louise who had twin ten-year-old boys. "Max looked forward to having children around," says Louise. "He took them fishing. He taught them to read star maps, to use his telescopes, and other things about astronomy. But I'm afraid the truth is they still don't appreciate him."

"I felt that part of our problem was crowding," explained Max. "We were living in an apartment where the boys shared a bedroom. We didn't have a yard. So we bought a house. But I don't think they appreciate that either. They leave everything a mess."

Some couples find that the children eventually warm up to their new stepparent. Others are content if their marriage is a happy one even if the stepparent-stepchild relationship is no more than a peaceful coexistence.

Yet the children's natural parent often carries the heaviest burden—guilt—as does Louise who says, "Sometimes I feel terribly sorry for Max. It's just not the same for him as having a new marriage and being able to be alone as much as we'd like. Nor does he have stepchildren who give him a great deal of pleasure. But this is my situation. I love him. I love them and we'll have to try to make the best of it."

Some stepparents who have no children of their own and whose stepchildren visit for weekends and vacations have special problems.

When Stepchildren Visit

"His relationship with Sarah and Michael is unnatural to start with," comments Marlene, a stepmother, about her husband, Martin. "He doesn't see them for a week or two weeks at a time and then when they do come, all his attention goes to them," she says. Does she resent it?

"I guess I resent it because it's so strained, so indulgent. I *never* get that much attention from him. And he doesn't say anything when they don't clean up the kitchen or leave their clothes all over the place."

Yet some of Marlene's resentment may stem from her own way of dealing with her stepchildren. "I will *never* discipline or scold them," she says. "I want them to like me and I don't want to upset Martin. If they leave things, I either go into my room until my blood pressure comes down or I go to their father. I'm not like my friend Elaine who will just say 'Look at this mess, clean it up' or 'leave me alone. I need some peace and quiet.' I can't do that. I keep it all inside."

Contrary to what Marlene may feel, most experts would advise her that discipline is important in her relationship with her stepchildren, that children need limits, and that they know discipline is a form of caring. And one psychiatrist talked about the fact that many women in Marlene's position are often afraid of making the children's father angry. "He has to think about her feelings as much as he would like her to think about *his* children's feelings. Then maybe they can get somewhere."

"A big problem comes up in the summer," says Marlene, a buyer in a department store. "We both are off

311

from our jobs for the month of August, and during *our* vacation, *we* get the kids. They go to camp in July and spend August with us, so the only parent who really gets a vacation is their mother. It's not their fault, I know," she adds, "but it doesn't seem fair."

"And another thing," Marlene added, "is that I always feel I have to be working because I don't want to be accused by the children or their mother of using money that should be going to them. I guess I'm very insecure. And the children sense it; they take advantage of me."

Marlene suggests to anyone who is contemplating marrying and becoming a stepparent that they keep certain important points in mind. "Understand: (1) That you will never have your spouse completely to yourself; (2) That he or she has a very big investment of *time* and *money* in the children (inheritance and property rights often become sticky issues); (3) Recognize that you may get all of the children at some point, *full-time*. (They may decide they want to live with you or don't want to live with the parent they're with, or their other parent may suddenly want them out); (4) Know yourself. If you have any qualms about children and the responsibility and work they entail, look for other options."

Concerns of Stepparents

While Marlene's feelings and those of many others like her are based on some very real difficulties which exist for stepparents, most especially for stepmothers who are usually at home with the children for more of the time than their husbands, a bit of her resentment may stem from a secret concern that she can't be as good a parent as if she were a natural parent and, therefore, all the responsibility is especially irritating.

Indeed, anthropologist Paul Bohannan and a research team at the Western Behavioral Science Institute found that to be the case when they conducted a study comparing stepchildren and stepfathers with natural children and their natural fathers for the National Institute of Mental Health.* They explained that the stepfathers "saw their youngsters as less happy than the natural fathers rated theirs . . . [and] also tended to view themselves as less effective than the natural fathers saw themselves . . . the mothers and children thought the stepfathers were just as good as the natural fathers but the stepfathers didn't believe it themselves."

Bohannan and his team further point out that "The stepchildren were, in general, just as happy and just as successful socially and academically as the children in natural families by their own testimony and that of their mothers . . . children tended to get along as well with their stepfathers as the other children did with their natural fathers."

In fact, Bohannan's research suggests something that should encourage stepfathers to take heart. According to his work, the *way* in which a father or stepfather handles his children has far more to do with the children's mental health, adjustment, and happiness than whether they are step- or natural fathers.

Bohannan and Erikson describe what they see as the

---

*Since women keep the children in the great majority of cases, most live-in stepparents are stepfathers and most of the limited research on stepparents done to date has focused on stepfathers.

four main categories of fathers which stepfathers or natural fathers are equally likely to fall into:

1. the Instrumental Father—who sees his major role as that of breadwinner and who spends little time with his family,
2. the Expressive Father who is concerned with the emotional aspects of family life and feels that a good father should spend a lot of time with his child,
3. the Autocratic Father whose main concern is enforcing the rules, and
4. the Patriarchal Father who is most concerned with providing a model of high competence and self-esteem. Healthiest children, according to the research of Bohannan and Erickson, are likely to be those of Expressive fathers.

A Vague Relationship

One troubling feature to many families of the stepchild-stepparent relationship is its ambiguousness and impermanence. There is no legal bond between stepparents and stepchildren, nor does any right to custody exist on the part of the stepparent (isolated cases of judges awarding custody to stepparents, in the child's best interests, have occurred but have been few). The lack of any clear incest taboo between stepparents and stepchildren can bring to mind thoughts of *Lolita* or *Desire Under the Elms*.

Some couples adopt in order to clarify the stepparent-stepchild relationship.

Adoption gives the stepchild a permanent legal tie to

his stepparent, with the same status as a natural child. In the event of a divorce, the child is fully entitled to child support. Adoption also establishes the incest taboo beyond a doubt.

The points favoring adoption notwithstanding, professionals say they're not at all sure it's a good idea.

"It depends on the reason for doing it," says Dr. Friedman. "If the stepparent is adopting out of his close feelings for the child and the child feels the same way, that's healthy. But if it's a matter of having the same name as a stepfather because of what the kids in school might say, that's not a very good reason."

Dr. Friedman and others point out that adoption has major drawbacks. In order for a stepchild to be adopted, his natural mother or father, whomever he is not living with, must give permission to let the child go, giving up all parental rights in the process. A child who claims he wants to be adopted perhaps because he wants to have the same name as his stepsisters and stepbrothers who go to the same school as he, may feel, on a deeper level, that his parent rejected and abandoned him if he actually does give his permission for adoption.

Not only does adoption cut a child off from his parent but it breaks his ties to some of his grandparents, aunts, uncles, and cousins.

If, on the other hand, a child has a weak relationship with his natural parent or no relationship at all, his stepparent wanting to adopt him can restore some of the loss of self-esteem he has suffered from what he probably sees as an abandonment by his natural parent.

There have been adoption cases, too, where a new wife has encouraged her husband to allow his natural children by a previous marriage to be adopted by their new stepfather, in part, in order to free the natural father from any further financial responsibility for the children.

Adoption is yet another area where parents can make the right decision only by thoughtfully considering the child's best interests.

For all the difficulties which each of the members of the growing number of combined families must overcome, and these shouldn't be downplayed, divorced parents are virtually flocking to the altar, often with their children beside them.[1] (Discounting the "hasty" remarriages which occur during the year immediately following divorce, the success rate for second marriages is high.) Morton and Bernice Hunt point out in their recent book, *The Divorce Experience,* that roughly "66 percent of first marriages of people in the twenty-five-to-thirty-five age range will last a lifetime and so will 62 percent of second marriages in the same age group." Again, eliminating hasty unions (often rebound marriages) would bring the survival rate for second marriages even higher. The reasons people are giving for remarrying indicate promise for success as well. In the Hunts' study, "companionship," "emotional needs," and "sexual needs" ranked as the first three reasons for remarrying, while the formerly more popular reasons—"financial security," "for the children's sake," and "to rejoin married society"—ranked far lower.

Hunt goes on to say, "Obviously, zero percent of those who were divorced the first time remained happy enough to stay in the marriage; but 62 percent of those people will stay married the second time."

Some adults actually find it easier with stepchildren than with their own children. Said one father, "I get the satisfactions but not the guilt."

His stepson added, "I like my family. I have one mother, one father, one stepmother, one stepfather, two grandmothers, one grandfather, one stepgrandmother, two brothers, a stepbrother and stepsister, and . . . a lot of others."

Chapter Twenty-Seven

LOOKING AHEAD

As adults put themselves and their children through the agonies of separation and divorce, they must wonder at the hidden traps of family life. Why does the family—the end of the rainbow, the heart of the American dream—so often disappoint? Do the same mistakes and the same pain lie ahead for the children?

The current divorce rate would suggest that families are becoming less stable and that our children run a high risk of suffering through divorce themselves. But perhaps we are missing some positive points.

Many parents who end their married life because they are demeaned, hurt, or saddened by it are demonstrating to their children the courage to admit painful truths, to take risks, and to change. And they are taking a stand against loveless marriages.

When today's divorcing couples reveal their deepest feelings, at least one member will usually say that they married for the wrong reasons—for security, because it was expected, or to be part of married society. What these couples may have argued about—the children, money, women's liberation, an extramarital affair, "not growing together"—were often only symptoms of a deeper deficiency in their relationships.

The hope for the family and for today's children lies in starting better marriages, in recognizing that the only valid standard for a marriage is mutual love, support and understanding.

Parents who face up to a bad marriage can be instructive in helping their children to be more careful and make better choices for themselves.

I hope this book has been helpful in alleviating some of the guilt and depression which parents sometimes feel following a separation and which can keep them and their children from moving on to happier, more satisfying lives.

NOTES

Chapter Two

1. Derdeyn, André P. "Child Custody Contests in Historical Perspective," *The American Journal of Psychiatry*, December, 1976. (People v. Humphries, 24 Bart 521 [NY 1857]).
2. Op. cit. (Brow v. Brightman, 136 Mass. 187 [Mass 1883]).
3. Op. cit. (Carr v. Carr, 22 Grat. 168 [Va. 1872]).
4. Op. cit. (Outer v. Outer, 120 SW 3d 203. [Mo. 1938]).
5. Finlay v. Finlay, 240 N.Y. 429, 148 N.E. 624 (1925).
6. Benedek, Elissa P., M. D. and Benedek, Richard S., J.D. "New Child Custody Laws: Making Them Do What They Say."
7. *New York Law Journal*; Nov. 29, 1977.

8. Stafford, Linley. "What's Hers Is Hers But His, Too." *The New York Times*, April 4, 1977.

Chapter Nine
1. Chiraboga, David, Ph.D. and Cutler, Loraine. "Stress Responses Among Divorcing Men and Women," *Journal of Divorce*, Vol. 1 (2) Winter 1977.

Chapter Ten
1. Judith S. Wallerstein, M.S.W. of the School of Social Welfare, University of California; Berkeley, California and Joan B. Kelly, Ph.D. of the Marin County Mental Health Center; San Rafael, California, have been investigators since 1971 on the long-term, extensive Children of Divorce Project. Parts of their research have appeared under the title "The Effects of Parental Divorce," in the *Journal of the American Academy of Child Psychiatry*, Vol. 14, No. 4, Autumn, 1975, and the *American Journal of Orthopsychiatry*, 46 (1) in Jan., 1976 and 46 (2) in April, 1976.

Chapter Eleven
1. In a survey conducted by the Foundation for Child Development, a New York research and policy group, psychologist and Project Director Dr. Nicholas Zill had a representative sampling of more than 2200 seven- to-ten-year-olds from intact as well as divorced families questioned in depth on a variety of subjects. It is interesting to note that 45 percent of *all* the children interviewed wished they could see their fathers more and a third missed their mothers as well.

Notes

2. Some other Fathers' Rights Organizations are:
   Families United for Equal Rights—New Jersey
   Men's Rights Association—Minnesota
   Equal Rights for Fathers—New York
   Fathers for Equal Rights, Wives and Grand-
      parents Coalition—Texas
   League for Human Rights in Divorce—South-
      ampton, New York
   Los Angeles Fathers for Equal Justice—Califor-
      nia
   Fathers United for Equal Justice—Cambridge,
      Mass.
   Divorced Men's Association of Connecticut—
      Connecticut

3. E. Mavis Hetherington of the University of
   Virginia and Martha Cox and Roger Cox of the
   DeJarnette Center for Human Development in
   Staunton, Virginia, found in their study of divorced fathers that one of the fathers' deepest
   concerns was the sense of loss over their children which some could not endure the pain from
   and reacted by pulling out of their children's
   lives.

Chapter Twelve
1. Hunter, Nan D. and Polikoff, Nancy D.,
   "Custody Rights of Lesbian Mothers: Legal Theory and Litigation Strategy." *Buffalo Law Review*,
   Vol. 25, 1976.

Chapter Nineteen
1. The poet Marya Mannes, in a speech at a New
   York State Conference on Marriage and Divorce,

commented that *all* women should build up their skills through training and courses. "Then if it (divorce) happens and a woman finds herself adrift at a certain age, she has the skills and resources to join the work force or to do something on her own."

Chapter Twenty-Six
1. On the question of whether to have children attend or participate in parents' weddings, experts advise, by all means, letting them take part to the extent that they would like to and feel comfortable doing so, but not forcing the child who, for a variety of reasons, would prefer not to.

RECOMMENDED READING FOR CHILDREN AND PARENTS

Blume, Judy. *It's Not the End of the World*. Bradbury Press.
4th-7th grade.

Catlin, Nancy. *The Single Parent*. Journal of Parents Without Partners, Inc.
For parents.

Gardner, Richard. *The Boys and Girls Book About Divorce*. Science House.
4th grade and up.

Gettleman, Susan & Markowitz, Janet. *The Courage to Divorce*. Simon and Schuster.
For parents.

Krantzler, Mel. *Creative Divorce*. M. Evans & Co.
For parents.

McHargue, Georgess. *Stoneflight*. Viking Press.
5th-8th grade.

Madison, Winifred. *Marinka, Katinka and Me (Susie)*. Bradbury Press.
2nd-4th grade.

Mann, Peggy. *My Dad Lives in a Downtown Hotel*. Doubleday.
3rd-6th grade.

Newfild, Marcia. *A Book for Jodan*. Atheneum.
3rd-5th grade.

Pevsner, Stella. *A Smart Kid Like You*. Seabury Press.
5th grade and up.

Richards, Arlene & Willis, Irene. *How to Get Together When Your Parents Are Coming Apart*. David McKay.
Young adults.

Smith, Doris. *Kick a Stone Home*. Crowell.
5th-9th grade.

Sitea, Linda. "Zachary's Divorce" in *Free to Be Me*. McGraw-Hill.
All ages.

Stoltz, Mary. *Leap Before You Look*. Harper & Row.
  7th grade and up.

Thomas, Ianthe. *Eliza's Daddy*. Harcourt Brace Jovano-
vich.
  Preschoolers and beginner readers.

BIBLIOGRAPHY

Benedek, Elissa P., M.D. and Benedek, Richard S., J.D. "New Child Custody Laws: Making Them Do What They Say," *American Journal of Orthopsychiatry*, 1972 (Oct.) Vol. 42 (5) 825-834.

Bohannan, Paul, and Erickson, R. "Stepping In." *Psychology Today*. January, 1978.

Corman, Avery. *Kramer vs. Kramer*, Random House, 1977.

Derdeyn, André P., M.D. "Child Custody Contests in Historical Perspective."

Despert, J.L. *Children of Divorce*. Doubleday, 1962.

Erikson, Erik H. *Childhood and Society*. W.W. Norton & Co., Inc., 1950.

Grote, Douglas F., M. Div., and Weinstein, Jeffrey P. "Joint Custody: A Viable and Ideal Alternative." *Journal of Divorce*, Vol. 1, No. 1, Fall 1977. Pp. 43-55.

Hunt, Morton and Hunt, Bernice. *The Divorce Experience,* McGraw-Hill, 1977.

Hunter, Nan D. and Polikoff, Nancy D. "Custody Rights of Lesbian Mothers: Legal Theory and Litigation Strategy," *Buffalo Law Review,* Vol. 25, 1976.

Kestenbaum, Clarice J. and Stone, Michael H. "The Effects of Fatherless Homes Upon Daughters: Clinical Impressions Regarding Paternal Deprivation." *Journal of the American Academy of Psychoanalysis,* 4(2): 171-190, 1976.

Kliman, Gilbert, M.D. *Psychological Emergencies of Childhood.* Grune & Stratton, 1968.

Orthner, Dennis. "Single-Parent Fatherhood," Department of Child Development and Family Relations. The University of North Carolina.

Stafford, Linley. "What's Hers Is Hers But His, Too," *The New York Times,* April 4, 1977.

Tooley, Kay, Ph.D. "Antisocial Behavior and Social Alienation Post Divorce." *American Journal of Orthopsychiatry.* 46 (1), January, 1976.

Wallerstein, Judith S., M.S.W. and Kelly, Joan, Ph.D. "The Effects of Parental Divorce," *American Journal of Orthopsychiatry* 46 (1), January 1976 and 46(2), April, 1976: "The Effects of Parental Divorce," *Journal of the American Academy of Child Psychiatry,* Vol. 14, No. 4, Autumn 1975.

Watson, Andrew S. "The Children of Armageddon: Problems of Custody Following Divorce." *Syracuse Law Review,* 1969: 21, 55-86.